Stuart,

    The author of this book is my cousin — Mom's sister's son. He's the scholar in our family. Enjoy!

        — Stt

TRUE GRIT

TRUE GRIT

CLASSIC TALES OF PERSEVERANCE

THEODORE PAPPAS

G2 entertainment

First published in the UK in 2018

© G2 Entertainment Limited 2018

Printed and bound in the UK.

ISBN 978-1782818144

Publisher: Jules Gammond
Designer: Heather Bowen

Our best endeavours have been made to secure copyright clearance for all photographs used, but in the event of any copyright owner being overlooked please go to www.G2ent. co.uk where you will find all relevant contact information. Photo Credits: Ruth Handler (BARBIE® and associated trademarks and trade dress are owned by and used with permission of Mattel, Inc. © All rights reserved); Dr. Seuss (by Al Ravenna, New York World-Telegram and the Sun Newspaper Photograph Collection/Library of Congress, Washington, D.C.); Joe Louis (1941 by Carl Van Vechten, Library of Congress, Washington, D.C.) and wartime poster (U.S. Government Printing Office); Walt Disney (from 1937 trailer to *Snow White and the Seven Dwarfs*) and with Mickey Mouse (by Harris & Ewing, Library of Congress, Washington, D.C.); Madeleine Albright (U.S. Department of State) and at the White House (U.S. Central Intelligence Agency); Thomas Edison (1922 by Louis Bachrach, Bachrach Studios, Library of Congress, Washington, D.C.) and photo with Henry Ford (Detroit Publishing Company, Library of Congress, Washington, D.C.); Clara Barton and Galveston disaster (Library of Congress, Washington, D.C.); Abraham Lincoln (1863 by Alexander Gardner) and on battlefield (both from the Library of Congress, Washington, D.C.); Marie Curie at Solvay Conference (by Benjamin Couprie); Ian Fleming (digital portrait by Paul Baack).

*For my children—Oliver,
Cecilia Jean, and Demetrius*

Contents

Grit: The Dark Underside of Achievement

How did the great men and women who changed the world actually do it? Were they simply smarter or more talented and privileged than the rest of us, enjoying higher IQs, superior educations, and better skills and connections? Was it just a matter of greater genius, talent, gifts, and opportunities?

Profiled in this book are ten of the most extraordinary men and women of the modern era. Their accomplishments are legendary, and their influence is visible in every country of the world. But apart from their historical significance and staggering influence, what else do these famed figures have in common? Anything? After all, as a group they seem a rather sundry lot. Their life stories are wildly different, in context and time, spanning multiple centuries, countries, and cultures. Their areas of expertise are equally diverse, ranging from science and invention (Thomas Edison and Marie Curie), politics and statecraft (Abraham Lincoln and Madeleine

Albright), and film and literature (Walt Disney, Ian Fleming, and Theodor Geisel) to sports (Joe Louis), business (Ruth Handler), and social outreach (Clara Barton). Even their backgrounds and personalities are highly dissimilar. Fleming, for example, was rich and privileged; Lincoln and Louis were poor, and Lincoln, Edison, and Disney suffered multiple bankruptcies. Disney was a high school dropout and the "addled" Edison was homeschooled; but Geisel, Albright, and Fleming enjoyed elite educations. Disney and Edison were physically beaten by their fathers; Albright and Fleming had parents who catered to their every need. Fleming, called "Glamour Boy," had good looks to accompany his great wealth; Lincoln was homely, Barton plain and plump and spoke with a lisp, and Louis stammered and was exceptionally shy; Disney, on the other hand, was an irrepressible extrovert with an infectious smile and personality.

So, other than their obvious skills and success in their respective fields, there would appear to be few ties that bind this seemingly random gathering of high achievers. But the qualities and characteristics that make something special—like the essence of a great wine, a classic film, or a dear friend—lie often below the surface, hidden from easy view, and the same is true for the individuals profiled here. For beneath the veneer of their famous accomplishments we find frequent battles with adversity, serial setbacks and defeats, and personal and professional hardships they endured along the way, and it's here—amid the dark underside of achievement that is seldom illuminated by our history books—that we find the special quality they possessed in common, that connects their life stories, and that paved their way to greatness and world influence: that life-changing mix of passion and perseverance popularly known as *grit*.

John Wayne won his sole Academy Award for his role as the in-trepid lawman in the classic western *True Grit*. This film, however, debuted in 1969 (the novel it's based on in 1968), and on any list of popular words in the half century since then *grit* would be a no-show—until recently. The word has made a remarkable comeback, as evidenced by several fine books. For example, in *Grit to Great: How Perseverance, Passion, and Pluck Take You from Ordinary to Extraordinary* (2015), Linda Kaplan Thaler and Robin Koval lambast the psychologists, teachers, and parents who for two generations, beneath the banner of the much-ballyhooed self-esteem movement, have taught children that self-confidence was their secret to success. The result, say the authors, has been a disaster: the grade inflation, the sense of entitlement among youth, and the celebration of mediocrity that is all too common today—the trophy-and-ribbon-for-every-runner mentality. "The whole self-esteem movement has been a flop, undermining the natural grit that this nation of immigrants brought with them in building a new life in a new land." But "there is the beginning of a backlash." Spurring this backlash, they suggest, was the 2012 commencement address at Wellesley High School by English teacher David McCullough, Jr. (son of Pulitzer Prize-winning historian David McCullough), a speech that quickly went viral. "You're not special," he bluntly told the students. "Contrary to what your U9 soccer trophy suggests, your glowing seventh-grade report card, despite every assurance of a certain corpulent purple dinosaur, that nice Mister Rogers and your batty Aunt Sylvia, no matter how often your maternal caped

crusader has swooped in to save you . . . you're nothing special."
What he urged them to understand is that "the fulfilling life, the
distinctive life, the relevant life, is an achievement, not something
that will fall into your lap because you're a nice person or Mommy
ordered it from the caterer. . . . The point is the same: get busy,
have at it. Don't wait for inspiration or passion to find you. Get
up, get out, explore, find it yourself and grab hold with both
hands."

"Passion and perseverance," the authors conclude, "matter more
than talent or intelligence when it comes to being successful. For
most of us, the corner office or professional kudos is the result of
hard work, rather than exceptional genes. The endgame, it turns
out, belongs to the truly diligent, not the merely talented. It belongs
to those who have *grit*."

Angela Duckworth sounds a similar note in *Grit: The Power of
Passion and Perseverance* (2016). Before becoming a psychologist
Duckworth was a teacher, and it was in the classroom that she too
began to detect a common element in the drive to succeed, one
she confirmed with analysis as a social scientist years later. Her
conclusion? Grit—hard work and stick-to-itiveness—as much as
talent, was key to success. Her message was "about the power of grit
to help you achieve your potential," because "what we accomplish
in the marathon of life depends tremendously on our grit—our
passion and perseverance for long-term goals." An overemphasis or
obsession with talent—IQ tests, "gifted programs" for our children,
etc.—merely "distracts us from that simple truth."

As the reader will see in the biographical profiles that follow, these ten masters of grit didn't simply *live* life but rather *pursued* it with the passion of a predator after prey. Not all of them were born with this consequential quality, but they acquired it over time and nurtured its growth, reminding us that grit, unlike innate talent and IQ, is a virtue that can be learned and cultivated. Despite personal inhibitions, they became bold, adventurous, take-charge types, self-directed and self-motivated, and staunch models of engagement who through force of will channeled their talents, ideas, and passion in meaningful ways, leaving an unmistakable and inspiring mark on the world. They heeded the ancient Greek instruction to "know thyself," and once they had discovered the inner dream, destiny, or vision of accomplishment that gave their life meaning, they set their compass by it and dedicated the whole of their efforts, over and over again, to realizing this future. What the sages of antiquity well understood we often now forget and almost never teach. "Virtues are formed in a man by his doing the actions," said Aristotle. Or as Will Durant more pithily put it, "We are what we repeatedly do. Excellence then is not an act but a habit."

Trailblazers at heart, these masters of grit were defiant before tradition, convention, and precedent, and instead of fearing and forgoing the road less traveled, they sought and even gained strength and inspiration from plodding the path unpaved and unpopular. They relished seeking the possible amid the improbable, finding answers to old problems long lingering as insolvable. Merely "going through the motions" was never a mirror of their lives, and ignoring their life mission or quitting in pursuit of it was never a serious long-term option. For them, inactivity was a toxin, and drifting rudderless at sea was a fate worse than drowning. For they constantly strove and stepped and worked and pushed on, and by staying engaged and in motion, literally and figuratively, physically and psychologically, they were able in the end to transcend their failures, cope with their struggles, overcome their disappointments, and successfully achieve their life's mission, changing the world in historic ways.

Even in the face of great physical limitations, they found a way to transform their liabilities into life-enhancing assets, as Edison and Lincoln especially did well. In this regard, these masters of grit were also masters of metamorphosis, very similar to the Stoic as defined by Nassim Nicholas Taleb, best-selling author of *The Black Swan: The Impact of the Highly Improbable* (2007): someone who "transforms fear into prudence, pain into transformation, mistakes into initiation, and desire into undertaking."

Whenever faced with great adversity—whether due to their own hand or to the hand of fate—these masters of grit could muster the courage to carry on with their life purpose intact, and such resilience and tenacity, like their passion, are what distinguished them from less successful players in their respective fields. They could "stumble from failure to failure with no loss of enthusiasm," for when they fell, they tried always to fall forward, and when they lost, they gleaned lessons from their failures that then could be leveraged for yet another assault on their goals. "Try again, fail again, fail better." Samuel Beckett's famed maxim could be their mantra.

Of course, these masters of grit were hardly paragons of virtue. High achievers are imperfect creatures like us all, and not every action by a hero is necessarily heroic. They are as blessed with virtues, strengths, and skills as tarnished with vices, weaknesses, and faults, and their shortcomings may even seem magnified in light of their staggering achievements. Any detailed look at the lives briefly surveyed in these pages will find their failings in high relief.

Indeed, many of the most successful and innovative leaders in the world could and can be highly unlikable at times—often brusque, abrasive, insensitive, and intolerant of anyone perceived as wasting their time and hindering their passionate pursuit of their goals. Steve Jobs comes readily to mind. Similarly, Barton and Handler could be pushy and bossy, Edison and Curie aloof and quite cold, and Geisel and Disney exacting and demanding. Edison's electrocution of animals as part of his experiments and public demonstrations is widely seen as monstrous today, and the marital infidelities of Louis, Fleming, and Geisel were hardly the acts of secular saints. But we needn't endorse the political party of Madeleine Albright or every wartime measure by Abraham Lincoln in order to appreciate their grit in the face of adversity and to gain from their life stories greater fortitude and forbearance in our own daily struggles. We need not *like* in order to *learn*.

Nor were these masters of grit immune to fears of failure or to moments of self-doubt. In fact, as the reader will see, quite a few of these individuals suffered repeated bouts of depression and "nervous breakdowns." They were all too human in this regard. But it was during these very times of crisis, when their character and convictions were challenged to the core, that they once again distinguished themselves. Rejecting the role of victim, they would never fully surrender to the devil of doubt or allow such a demon to haunt them for long. They refused to be permanently disabled by defeat, paralyzed by self-pity, or derailed from pursuing the destiny that brought meaning to their lives. They understood that scars are a sign of where we have been, not where we are going, and so through all the setbacks and disappointments they encountered, they could tap an inner strength, a special resolve, and find that critical reason to get up the next morning and trudge on in pursuit of their life's mission.

And though their focus on the future was firm, it was never fixed and incapable of strategic shifts. For they realized that even the chief element of their strategy for success—perseverance—could have a tipping point beyond which it facilitates neither victory nor happiness but impedes needed change, skirting ever close to the popular definition of insanity: "Doing the same thing over and over again and expecting different results." Like Kenny Rogers' gambler, they knew when to hold 'em, knew when to fold 'em.

In the end, we find in the lives of these masters of grit the locus of the human capacity to rebound and push on. Their passion to succeed, their singleness of purpose in the face of repeated failure, and the sense of urgency with which they lived their lives can inspire us all, renewing hope and faith in our own ability to endure, to succeed, and even to change the world in our own special way.

On a personal note, allow me to thank three long-time Britannica colleagues—Robert Lewis, Tom Panelas, and Dale Hoiberg—for their kind and constructive reading of this manuscript, in part or in full.

Ruth Handler

Born: November 4, 1916, Denver, Colorado
Died: April 27, 2002, Los Angeles, California

CHAPTER 1

The Spur of Humiliation

Ruth "Barbie Doll" Handler

Her 40th birthday party in 1999 was held at the Waldorf-Astoria hotel in New York, and the guest list was as stunning as the posh surroundings. Hosted by music legend Dick Clark, the attendees included Jackie Joyner-Kersee, the Olympic gold medalist; Vera Wang, the famed fashion designer; Ann Moore, president of *People* magazine; entertainment executive Geraldine Laybourne, creator of Nickelodeon; Muriel Siebert, the first woman to own a seat on the New York Stock Exchange; and Sylvia Earle, called "Her Deepness" by the *New York Times,* a "Living Legend" by the Library of Congress, and a "Hero for the Planet" by *Time* magazine for her pioneering work in oceanography; there was even an unveiling of special artwork by acclaimed photographer Annie Leibovitz. The entire event, which included a tribute to each of these "Ambassadors of Dreams" who "encourage and inspire young women of the new millennium," teaching them that "no goal is unattainable," was living proof of how successful the women's movement had been in nurturing and acknowledging achievements by women. And yet, the honoree whom these women leaders had gathered to celebrate was the American icon most hated by feminist activists, an idol accused of everything from spurring sexism, consumerism, and "body dysmorphic disorders" to destroying self-esteem in young girls. The object of their scorn was puny and plastic but oh-so powerful: the 11½-inch "birthday girl," Barbie.

Barbie's creator, Ruth Handler—who started the Mattel toy company with her husband and a partner in 1945 and who launched Barbie in 1959—never accepted this pejorative, "anti-woman" interpretation of her famed doll. In fact, Ruth saw Barbie as a female pioneer and early feminist of sorts, as a confident, single woman whose endless career possibilities (some 150 to date) taught young ladies that they had choices and didn't need a husband to define their worth or role in life. This sense of self-sufficiency was a revolutionary notion in the gender-restrictive days of the 1950s, as first-generation Barbie owner M.G. Lord noted in *Forever Barbie* (1994):

> [Barbie] didn't teach us to nurture, like our clinging, dependent Betsy Wetsys and Chatty Cathys. She taught us independence. Barbie was her own woman. She could invent herself with a costume change: sing a solo in the spotlight one minute, pilot a starship the next. She was Grace Slick and Sally Ride, Marie Osmond and Marie Curie. She was all that we could be . . .

The idea of an *adult doll* for girls dawned on Ruth while watching her daughter Barbara (for whom Barbie was named) play with her friends. Ruth noticed that, as the girls grew older, they began to shun the "baby dolls" in diapers and infant clothes and to gravitate toward "paper dolls," which they could dress in adult outfits and imagine in more grown-up situations. "They were using the dolls to project their . . . own futures as adult woman," noted Ruth. But paper dolls were flimsy and uninspiring, which meant one thing to the ever-entrepreneurial Ruth: a market opportunity. "If only we could take this play pattern and three-dimensionalize it, we would have something very special," she said, and that "something very special" would be Barbie—the most successful toy in history.

Ruth's idea of an adult-proportioned doll for kids seemed outrageous in its day. "Ruth, no mother is going to buy her daughter a doll with breasts," said her husband, and the other male executives at Mattel agreed. But a non-shapely doll seemed ridiculous to Ruth, especially for the market she was aiming for. "Every little girl needed a doll through which to project herself into her dream of her future," argued Ruth. "If she was going to do role playing of what she would be like when she was 16 or 17, it was a little stupid to play with a doll that had a flat chest. So I gave it beautiful breasts."

Not helping Ruth's case was the doll on which she planned to model Barbie: the Bild Lilli, a racy gag doll for guys based on a sexy and sassy German cartoon character. But the doll's bawdy background mattered little to Ruth, who ingeniously zeroed in on what no one else saw—how the doll could be toned down and, amazingly, even sold to children. Such was Ruth's marketing genius.

How and where to produce the product proved a daunting challenge, and ultimately it was only in Japan that Ruth could find the craftsmen capable of manufacturing at a reasonable price point a doll with the malleable features and miniature custom-sized clothing that Ruth envisioned for her product. But concerns over the doll continued at Mattel, especially after the prototype arrived from Japan sporting not only breasts but . . . *nipples*! Even Ruth agreed that such realism was unacceptable, but once the offending protuberances had been filed off, the project proceeded apace.

Selling her husband and Mattel on the doll was one thing, but selling it to the toy industry and the public was quite another. When

Ruth Handler, creator of the Barbie doll, with her husband, Elliot, c. 1968.

Barbie was presented to mothers in a private market study in 1958, the moms were outraged and roundly rejected her. Barbie fared no better when she made her public debut, wearing a zebra-striped bathing suit and stiletto heels, at the New York Toy Fair on March 9, 1959. "The male buyers thought we were out of our minds because of the breasts, and it was a male-dominated business," remembered a Mattel employee cited by biographer Robin Gerber in *Barbie and Ruth*. "For the most part, the doll was hated." Ruth, the hard-as-nails, tough-talking company president—her rich font of billingsgate could make a sailor blush—didn't cry often, but she cried that evening, and she cried very hard.

But once the shock of the failed debut had worn off, Ruth doubled down on her effort to bring Barbie to market—quitting was not an option. A new strategy, however, was clearly needed, and the one she fashioned proved just as revolutionary as her product: she would boldly bypass Barbie's two major impediments—i.e., moms and the male-dominated distribution channels—and appeal directly to the consumer, meaning young girls themselves. To achieve this, Ruth cleverly tapped the budding medium of television, where Mattel was the first company to advertise toys on a year-round basis and the first to create commercials oriented specifically for kids, not their toy-buying parents. (This marketing scheme seems obvious today—hook the young girls, and you've hooked their mothers' pocketbook—but it was a bold and innovative strategy in its day.) In fact, Ruth's commercials portrayed Barbie less like a toy—seldom is Barbie even called a doll—and more like a real young lady, one adorned with makeup and shot like a professional model. Ruth's reward for her groundbreaking efforts? Further ridicule. "Can you believe what that crazy Mattel did?" remarked the wife of the president of another company. "They went on TV and expected moms to buy whore-looking dolls for their kids."

Undaunted, Ruth ignored the pillory, persevered, and pushed on, confident that her three-year investment in Barbie—in time, money, and tears—was not in vain. And like a slowly but surely simmering fuse, the sales explosion that Ruth had hoped for finally occurred. By the fall of 1959, young girls, their mothers, and cha-grined toy-sellers nationwide were scrambling to get their hands on that "whore-looking doll." Some 350,000 Barbies were sold the first year, and it would take Mattel three additional years—and eventually a city-size army of Japanese workers (some 10,000 of them)—to catch up with demand. More than a half-century later, Mattel remains a billion-dollar company, with a Barbie reportedly sold every two or three seconds somewhere in the world.

By the end of the 1960s, Ruth and Mattel could seemingly do no wrong, as even their non-Barbie products, such as Hot Wheels miniature cars, had become global sensations. But all this changed in the 1970s. Unwisely following advice to expand and diversify into non-toy industries, such as pet products, playground equip-ment, and even a circus (Ringling Brothers), Mattel expanded exponentially and divided into divisions with more and more distant management structures that lay beyond anything Ruth could possibly keep up with, and with this rapid, global expansion came executives with questionable accounting practices to help

"I'm not sure I would have grown much had I not lived through such grief. I think there's nothing like adversity to make one grow."

RUTH HANDLER

the company through the economic downturns of the early 1970s. These financial irregularities soon attracted the attention of the Securities and Exchange Commission, and in a mandated corporate restructuring in 1975, Ruth and her husband suffered the ultimate humiliation: they were removed from their own company. Ruth, as the former company president, was personally charged with various fraud-related crimes. Although steadfastly proclaiming her innocence, Ruth pleaded no contest and was fined and sentenced to 2,500 hours of community service.

The cancer on the corporate body of Mattel was bad enough, but an actual malignancy had developed within Ruth as well. Diagnosed with breast cancer in 1970, she underwent a modi-fied radical mastectomy, leaving her scarred both physically and mentally, in constant pain, and unable (she believed) to manage her company adequately when it needed her most. Humbled and humiliated in public and in private, broken in health as well as in spirit, and laboring under the shadow of financial irregularities if not illegalities, Ruth struggled to come to terms with the radical changes in her life. But despite the adversity and the severity of her troubles, wallowing in despair would never be an acceptable long-term option for Ruth; it wasn't in the wake of Barbie's disastrous debut, and it wouldn't be now. So once the shock of these staggering developments had worn off—and by no means would it wear off easily—Ruth charted a new course for herself, one spawned by her personal and professional misfortunes and made possible by her resilience and grit, and the new career she fashioned for the second half of her life would not only rebuild her reputation in the business world but also help countless women, and herself, in the process.

As Ruth knew firsthand, breast cancer in 1970 was a woman's "secret shame," a "humiliation" that was often suffered in silence and hidden from even family and friends. This culture of shame began to crumble in 1974, when First Lady Betty Ford talked openly about her mastectomy, and it suffered another blow when writer Susan Sontag tackled the issue (and the victim-blaming "cancer personality" so widely cited as a source of the disease at that time) in her classic *Illness as Metaphor* (1978). It was this war on the social stigma surrounding the disease that Ruth joined in a unique way in 1975.

Feeling disfigured, unfeminine, and unattractive after her surgery, Ruth searched in vain for a good prosthetic breast to fill out her figure and help restore her self-esteem. Finding one was no easy task. Some of her doctors callously told her just to use her old bras and to stuff the empty side with rolled-up stockings or discarded gloves; others pointed to the few prosthetics then on the market—hard, ill-fitting blobs designed by men with little understanding of the nuances of a woman's body, its balance, and true dimensions.

Outraged but not discouraged, Ruth stepped in to fill the void. With the same passion with which she had conceived and produced Barbie, she created a company called Ruthton, whose aim was the production of a line of custom-sized, realistic-feeling prosthetic breasts called Nearly Me. Her goal for the new product was the same as her goal for the eternally-single, career-oriented Barbie: to show women (in this case, breast cancer survivors for whom reconstructive surgery was not a feasible, desired, or immediate option) that they had choices. One of Ruth's first customers? Betty Ford.

If eyebrows were raised at Ruth's novel marketing of Barbie, jaws now dropped with her selling of Nearly Me. For during presentations around the country and even on television, Ruth would brazenly invite men to feel her breasts, to squeeze and poke them, all in an effort to find the "fake" one. She'd then rip open her blouse, proudly displaying an attractive, prosthetic-filled bra, and remove the artificial breast for everyone to inspect. Ruth's shock-and-awe tactics made for good marketing, but, more importantly, they were orchestrated specifically to help break down the stigma associated with discussing cancer and to rid "mastectomees" (a term she coined for mastectomy patients like herself) of any sense of shame. As Ruth and her retailers would repeatedly say, "She's lost a part of her body. She hasn't committed a crime."

"For many women, Nearly Me had made Ruth a saint," wrote biographer Robin Gerber, "but Barbie had made her a star." Ruth had her own, unique take on the career arc of her life: "I've gone from breast to breast."

Although more heartache would lay ahead for Ruth, as her only son Kenneth (for whom Barbie's boyfriend Ken was named) would die in 1994 after contracting another closeted disease—AIDS, she was able in her final years through her many struggles and misfortunes to find and enjoy a deeper appreciation for life, and for this she was most grateful.

She was also eternally grateful for the creation that had fundamentally changed her life and the face of consumer culture—Barbie. Her deep pride in her product lives on in the brand. When Barbie was chosen by *Sports Illustrated* to appear alongside world-class models in its 50th anniversary swimsuit edition in 2014, wearing an updated version of the famed zebra-striped one-piece that she had worn in 1959, Mattel took to social media both to publicize the event to Barbie's millions of fans and to preempt the sniping of her ardent critics. The Twitter hashtag Mattel chose for its PR campaign was the perfect embodiment of Ruth's bold and defiant spirit: #Unapologetic.

Theodor Seuss Geisel

Born: March 2, 1904, Springfield, Massachusetts
Died: September 24, 1991, La Jolla, California

CHAPTER 2

The Maddening Wait
for Opportunity

Theodor "Dr. Seuss" Geisel

At the Lollapalooza rock festival in Providence, Rhode Island, in August 1994, Microsoft cofounder Paul Allen erected a circus tent called the Electric Carnival. Packed with colorful computers and cool-looking monitors, the exhibit offered the music fans something seemingly new: a chance, through software called the "Baby Maker," to combine their images to see what their potential offspring would look like. What most folks in attendance didn't realize was that the idea behind these progeny pictures was not a new one, and that a contraption called the "Infantograph" was conceived in 1938 that promised the same results, albeit via a non-digital camera that superimposed images of the prospective parents over an outline of a baby's face. The inventor conceived the idea while he walked home from the subway in Manhattan, and "it was a stroke of genius so brilliant," he said, "that I almost fell into a steaming Con-Edison manhole." Certain that the invention would make him a millionaire, he patented the idea, formed a corporation, and with a partner built a prototype, all in preparation for launching the product at the 1939 New York World's Fair; he had even written the ad copy to be used at the fair: "If You Married That Gal You're Walking With, What Would Your Children Look Like? Come In And Have Your Infantograph Taken!" With seemingly everything set, there remained but one problem: the contraption didn't work. The superimposed images would seldom align correctly, leaving the babies with crooked noses and sometimes even mustaches. The entire effort, in other words, was a colossal flop. In time, the inventor would indeed make millions, but his fortune and fame would hail not from a camera but from his inimitable words and illustrations. "It was my finest failure," said Theodor Seuss Geisel, better known to the world by his pen name, Dr. Seuss.

The years preceding this ill-conceived effort had been successful ones for Geisel. He had received a first-rate education, attending Dartmouth College from 1921-25 and then spending the following year at Oxford, where he studied the works of Jonathan Swift and considered pursuing a doctorate and becoming a scholar. But once his class notebooks at Oxford filled up with more doodles than details about English literature, it became clear that his future would take a different path. In fact, it was during his college days that "Seuss" made his first appearance in print. It seems, after getting caught with bootleg gin during his senior year at Dartmouth (when Prohibition was in full swing), he lost his editorship of the campus humor magazine where he published his cartoons. To circumvent this literary quarantine, Ted (as friends and family called him) started publishing his work under a pseudonym, "Seuss." This "corny subterfuge," as he coined it, continued after college, when he published cartoons under the name "Dr. Theophrastus Seuss" in 1927 and simply "Dr. Seuss" in 1928. The honorific "Dr.," he explained, was compensation for the doctorate he never earned at Oxford. And as for publishing under his real name of "Geisel"? He was saving that, he claimed, for the Great American Novel he would someday write.

Upon returning to the States and moving to New York in 1927, he soon settled into a solid career. Through his magazine cartoons, humorous essays, and work on major advertising campaigns for large companies such as Standard Oil, he quickly made a name for himself in the late 1920s and 30s as a New York ad-man and illustrator; his tagline for an insecticide pump, "Quick, Henry, the Flit!," was featured in advertisements for nearly two decades and became a national catchphrase, used in mock emergencies, even becoming a staple of comedy routines on stage and radio. Geisel had also produced the captivating drawings for a popular "collection of schoolboy wisdom" (i.e., examination mistakes) called *Boners*, which became a *New York Times* best-seller in 1931. (Cartooning and advertising copy would remain Geisel's prime source of income into the 1950s.)

So life was good for Geisel in the 1930s. He enjoyed a solid income, was traveling the world, and had secured a plush Park Avenue apartment—few could boast of better perks during the depths of the Depression. It would have been all too easy for someone in his position to grow comfortable in the moment, become complacent, and allow any higher aspirations to wither on the vine; after all, there is often nothing more lethal to ambition than success. But complacency and Geisel were never good

"Oh, the things you can find,

If you don't stay behind."

DR. SEUSS

bedfellows, and so he followed instead the advice he would soon be offering kids the world over:

> You have brains in your head.
> You have feet in your shoes.
> You can steer yourself any direction you choose.

And the direction he steered toward was his own, unique brand of children's literature. Geisel always said he wrote children's stories because that was the only kind of freelance writing not forbidden by his corporate advertising contracts. But there may have been a deeper, more personal reason: it was shortly after a surgery had left his wife incapable of bearing children that he attempted his first kids' story (an unpublished ABC book), and a desire to see what his offspring might have looked like is perhaps also what inspired the Infantograph. "You have 'em, I'll amuse 'em" became his pat answer whenever asked how a childless man could write so well for children. But this likely was just his offhand way of skirting a painful, uncomfortable subject. "It was not that we didn't want to have children," he'd later confess. "That wasn't it."

Geisel's first book, *A Story That No One Can Beat*, seemed hardly true: the story was actually *easy* to beat—because no one would publish it. As Judith and Neil Morgan report in their fine biography of Seuss, 27 publishers rejected it in 1936-7. His work, he was told, was "too different"; his versifying not "in vogue"; and he failed to deliver a strong enough "message or moral" for transforming young readers into "good citizens." This last objection infuriated Geisel, who would thunder to his wife: "What's wrong with kids having fun reading without being preached at?"

On the day of his 27th rejection, as he told the story, he decided to throw in the towel, to give up on his stillborn career as a children's writer, and to burn his dog-eared manuscript. But then destiny struck with a different plan. An old friend from Dartmouth just happened to notice Geisel walking grimly along Madison Avenue with manuscript under arm. As fate would have it, the old friend had just three hours earlier been named the new editor for children's literature at Vanguard Press. He invited Geisel up to his office, he and his colleagues read Geisel's manuscript, and . . . the rest is history.

Geisel understood that this fortuitous meeting on the street was the sheerest of luck. But it was just as true that his doggedness and grit in the face of near constant disappointment had left him

Dr. Seuss at work in 1957 on a drawing of the Grinch, the hero of his forthcoming book, *How the Grinch Stole Christmas!*

in a position to answer the proverbial door when opportunity came a-knocking. For had he given up sooner—maybe after his 25th rejection, or even the 26th—he perhaps never would have experienced that chance encounter that changed his life. Or as he liked to put it, "If I had been going down the other side of Madison Avenue, I'd be in the dry-cleaning business today."

Geisel's book, published under a new title, *And to Think That I Saw It on Mulberry Street*, appeared in late 1937. Dedicated to the wife of his old Dartmouth friend who made the book possible and with the story's narrator named after their son, the book introduced for the first time to a wide audience the unique rhythm and rhyme now synonymous with Dr. Seuss:

> And that is a story that no one can beat,
> When I say that I saw it on Mulberry Street.

The reviews of the book were lavish in their praise. The *Atlantic Monthly* said it was "so completely spontaneous that the American child can take it to his heart on sight." Beatrix Potter, creator of Peter Rabbit, called it in a private letter "the cleverest book I have met with for many years," praising the fact that it bucked the trend of so "many story books for children [that] are condescending." Geisel took enormous pride in his ability to communicate with kids without condescension. "I don't write for children. I write for people," he said. "Ninety percent of the children's books patronize the child and say there's a difference between you and me, so you listen to this story. I, for some reason or another, don't do that. I treat the child as an equal." In fact, children were not only equal in his eyes but even better than adults in one way. "I'd rather write for kids," he famously quipped. "They're more appreciative; adults are obsolete children, and the hell with them."

But the most important review of Geisel's inaugural tale was also the shortest, the one that issued from the pen of the famed critic Clifton Fadiman at *The New Yorker.* Fadiman sagely discerned the rare and budding genius reflected in the debut book before him, and he zeroed in, with a single sentence, on the masterful twofold way that Dr. Seuss cast his spell over children and parents alike. Geisel could reportedly recite word for word, until the day he died, the Fadiman review that helped launch and solidify his literary career: "They say it's for children, but better get a copy for yourself and marvel at the good Dr. Seuss' impossible pictures and the moral tale of the little boy who exaggerated not wisely but too well."

Like most cartoonists and illustrators, Geisel lent his talents to the war effort during World War II. In the early years of the conflict he published hundreds of cartoons in a progressive tabloid newspaper in New York, *PM,* where he lambasted America First isolationists like Charles Lindbergh, and after the United States entered the war in the wake of the Pearl Harbor attack in December 1941, he designed morale-boosting posters for the Treasury Department and War Production Board and wrote propaganda and training films for director Frank Capra's unit in the U.S. Army Signal Corps. As part of his film work, Geisel was sent to Europe in the fall of 1944, where in Luxembourg he happened upon the former editor of *PM,* now an officer in army intelligence. As recounted by Seuss biographer Caroline M. Smith, his old boss sent him off with a military police escort to a "quiet sector," Bastogne, along the Belgian border, to give him a taste of "some fighting." Unfortunately, Geisel and his escort got off course and ended up ten miles behind enemy lines. It wasn't a good time to get lost—the Germans suddenly launched a massive counterattack on the Allies, their last major offensive on the Western Front. Unbeknownst to Geisel and his escort, they had driven smack into the Battle of the Bulge. Three harrowing nights followed before their rescue by British troops. Without a soldierly bone in his body, the lanky "Captain Geisel" did carry a weapon, a .45 revolver, but he was such a horrible shot that he figured his best chance for surviving any encounter with enemy soldiers was to "grab it by the barrel and throw it." As he later joked, "Nobody came along and put up a sign saying, *This is the Battle of the Bulge. How was I supposed to know?*" Two of Geisel's wartime films later won Academy Awards as documentaries: *Your Job in Germany* (1945) was re-released as *Hitler Lives* (directed by the great Don Siegel of *Invasion of the Body Snatchers* and *Dirty Harry* fame) and won a 1945 Academy Award, and *Our Job in Japan* (1945) was the basis for *Design for Death*, which won a 1947 Academy Award.

It was in the 1950s, however, when Geisel really hit his stride. His full-time job remained in advertising, at least for the moment, but his passion was children's literature, and his decades of perseverance were about to pay off, and pay off big—to the tune of $500 million in book royalties over his lifetime.

The decade started out with yet another Academy Award, when Geisel's 1950 film *Gerald McBoing-Boing* won the Oscar for best animated short subject. What followed then was the string of literary classics which made Dr. Seuss world famous and which will likely never fall from favor or mind, including *Horton Hears a Who!* (1954), *The Cat in the Hat* (1957), *How the Grinch Stole Christmas! (1957), One Fish Two Fish Red Fish Blue Fish* (1960), *Green Eggs and Ham* (1960), *Hop on Pop* (1963), *Fox in Socks* (1965), *The Foot Book* (1968), *The Lorax* (1971), and *Oh, the Places You'll Go!* (1990). Nor will readers soon forget the classic tales inspired by Geisel. After the stunning success of *The Cat in the Hat*—a million copies had sold by 1960—Geisel, his wife, and Phyllis Cerf of Random House founded Beginner Books for early readers. Two of the line's earliest books were the classic *Go, Dog, Go!* (1961) by Philip D. Eastman and *The Big Honey Hunt* (1962) by Stanley and Janice Berenstain, the first of the popular Berenstain Bears book.

By the mid-1960s Geisel had become one of the most popular writers in the world. He had achieved a success beyond his wildest dreams, and the person at his side every step of the way—from his failures and frustrations in the 1930s to his great fame and fortune in the 1950s and 60s—had been his loving wife, Helen Palmer. Helen was a talented writer and children's author in her own right, co-writing with Ted the Oscar-winning documentary *Design for Death*. But by the mid-1960s, Ted had begun to chafe at the single-mindedness of her work on his career—as collaborator and critic, editor and business manager—and when combined with her worsening health issues—ulcers, partial paralysis, and Guillain-Barré syndrome—their relationship reached the breaking point. With his marriage at a crossroads, Ted found solace in the arms of another woman. Despondent and bereft of hope and in constant pain, and never wanting to be a burden to Ted or a drain on his career, Helen took her own life in 1967. As noted by the Morgans in their biography of Ted, the suicide was perceived as an act of love, as Helen's final selfless gift to the man she adored. "I love you so much," she wrote in a letter left for Ted. "I am too old and enmeshed in everything you do and are, that I cannot conceive of life without you. . . . My going will leave quite a rumor but you can say I was overworked and overwrought. Your reputation with your friends and fans will not be harmed." Ted was devastated. All of the powers he had mustered to persevere in his professional life were now needed more than ever to survive on the home front. "I didn't know whether to kill myself, burn the house down, or just go away and get lost," he said. But get lost he did—lost in his work. Like many of the individuals profiled in these pages, he turned to work as a salve for heartache and tragedy—to cope, to heal, to restore order to his world, to re-engage with the normalcy of everyday life.

Geisel's celebrity continued to grow in the 1970s, and lifetime achievement awards followed for him in the 1980s. In 1984 he won a special Pulitzer Prize "for his contribution over nearly half a century to the education and enjoyment of America's children and their parents," and in 1985 Princeton University declared him an honorary Doctor of Fine Arts for showing children "the way to the adult world, as he shows adults the way to the child." But perhaps the most meaningful "doctorate" Geisel ever received was the medical one afforded him by *Time* magazine upon his death in 1991, when its obituary declared him "one of the last doctors to make house calls—some 200 million of them in 20 languages, [reaching] a unique and hallowed place in the nurseries of the world."

Madeleine Albright

Born: May 15, 1937, Prague, Czechoslovakia

CHAPTER 3

Warring From the Outside
Madeleine Albright

"**S**orry, Madeleine, you don't get one of the books." The book in question, as she explained to Michael Shelden of the London *Telegraph*, outlined emergency measures for presidential succession, and she would never get a copy because her foreign birth disqualified her from ever becoming U.S. president. Over the course of her long and storied life, it wasn't the first time nor the last time that Madeleine Albright—U.S. ambassador to the United Nations (1993–97), the first female U.S. secretary of state (1997–2001), and the highest-ranking woman then to serve in the U.S. government—had felt like an outsider.

Madeleine and her family had fled their native Czechoslovakia in March 1939, just days after Hitler's invasion of their country. By fleeing, they had escaped arrest and likely relocation to a concentration camp, where two dozen of Madeleine's Jewish relatives, including three of her grandparents, would perish. Like thousands of European refugees, they spent the war in England, where they endured the German bombings of London before relocating to the outskirts of town for greater safety. While in England her father worked for the Czech government-in-exile. He also, as a buffer against future persecution, converted the family to Catholicism, and only as an adult would Madeleine learn of her Jewish roots. After the war, the family returned to Czechoslovakia and then moved to Belgrade, Yugoslavia, where Madeleine's father served as the Czech ambassador. In Belgrade, however, they faced another tyrannical foe, communism, and to protect Madeleine from the Marxist indoctrination common in Yugoslav schools, she was tutored at home and then sent to a private institution in Switzerland, where she mastered French and changed her name from Marie Jana to Madeleine. But with the Soviet-sponsored communist coup in Czechoslovakia in 1948, Madeleine and her family became refugees once again. This time they fled to the United States, where her father landed a position teaching international relations at the University of Denver. There an institution is now named in his honor—the Josef Korbel School of International Studies. Among her father's star students was another ambitious young lady with an interest in foreign policy, someone later inspired by Madeleine's own pioneering career: Condoleezza Rice, the second female U.S. secretary of state (2005-09) and the first black female to hold the post.

The resilience that the Korbel family exhibited throughout their tumultuous history was ingrained in Madeleine, and so whenever facing adversity or exclusion—as in the incident above, when she didn't as U.S. secretary of state "get one of the books"—she had a strong familial history of patience and perseverance to draw on.

Upon resettling in Denver, Madeleine did what the Korbels had become expert at doing: assimilating to the surroundings of their latest adopted land. To Madeleine, this meant trying to be "an average American" and learning to speak English without an accent—not Czech, not French, not British. After a private secondary school education, Madeleine attended and graduated from Wellesley College in Massachusetts, where she studied political science. During a summer internship at the *Denver Post*, she met and fell in love with the affluent scion of a newspaper empire, Joseph Medill Patterson Albright. (His grandfather had founded the *New York Daily News*, his great-great grandfather had owned the *Chicago Tribune* and been mayor of Chicago, and his aunt, Alicia Patterson, had founded and edited *Newsday*.)

This was a time in American history when female college students were expected to follow up their B.A. or B.S. with their Mrs., and Madeleine did just that—she married Albright right after graduating from Wellesley in 1959. It was then, in the early 1960s, as Madeleine juggled her roles as wife of a peripatetic journalist and socially prominent media heir, mother of three daughters, and continuing student of international relations (taking graduate classes at Johns Hopkins University and eventually mastering five languages) that she was once again reminded of her "outsider status." This uneasy feeling was especially evident one night at a house party in D.C., where her husband Joe was now covering the State Department for *Newsday*. As remembered by writer Ward Just and recounted in Michael Dobbs' *Madeleine Albright:*

"I was taught to strive not because there were any guarantees of success but because the act of striving is in itself the only way to keep faith with life."

MADELEINE ALBRIGHT

A Twentieth-Century Odyssey, Joe and his Georgetown buddies were engaged in one of their favorite pastimes: debating which of them would be first to make the cover of *Time* magazine. As the discussion heated up, Joe suggested that Madeleine excuse herself and fetch the men another bottle of wine. It was a small matter, a common slight reflective of the *Mad Men*-like gender roles of the day. But never did it dawn on anyone that evening that the only person in the room who would ever grace *Time*'s cover would be Madeleine. "I felt that I was facing a double hardship," she later noted. "I was a woman, and I was a foreigner."

When once asked to name the chief obstacle she ever encountered as a woman cultivating a high-powered position in a male-dominated field, she said: "Proving it could be done." And proving it not just at home but abroad as well. When Albright's motorcade was stoned by Serbian rebels in 1997, during her tenure as U.S. secretary of state, it was telling that they did so while shouting, "Bitch!"

So despite the limited opportunities and encouragements then offered "career women"—"No responsible person in America would suggest that young women curtail that most important of careers—homemaking," said U.S. Secretary of Defense Neil McElroy in his commencement address at Madeleine's 1959 Wellesley graduation—Madeleine pushed on with her personal career interests nonetheless. After a short stint as a picture editor and publicity assistant at Encyclopædia Britannica in Chicago, where Joe was working for the *Chicago Sun-Times*, she set her sights on the

professional track that would change her life—government, politics, and international affairs. (When, during her job interview at
Britannica, the male executives inquired about when she planned
on getting pregnant, a common and perfectly legal interview question at that time, she memorably replied according to company
lore, "Not at this moment, thank you." As she recalled in her 2003
autobiography, *Madame Secretary: A Memoir*, "I can't remember
being offended [by the question]; I just said I wasn't in a hurry.")

Pursuing her own interests wasn't easy, however, as Joe shut-
tled between jobs in New York and Washington and she dutifully
followed as mother and wife. But she began nonetheless, ever
so slowly, to lay the foundation of a career outside of the home.
She licked stamps for Robert Kennedy's senatorial campaign in
1964; attended Columbia University in the late 1960s, earning her
master's degree in 1968; worked for Senator Edmund Muskie on
his presidential campaign in 1972, earning a reputation as a stellar
fundraiser; received her Ph.D. in public law and government from
Columbia University in 1976; was appointed to the staff of President
Jimmy Carter's National Security Council in 1978, recommended
to the post by her Columbia mentor, Zbigniew Brzezinski, Carter's
national security advisor; landed a teaching position at Georgetown
University and its prestigious School of Foreign Service in 1982; and
served as foreign policy adviser to Walter Mondale and Michael
Dukakis on their presidential runs in 1984 and 1988, respectively.

These opportunities provided Madeleine with invaluable experience, but they produced just as many failures and frustrations.
Most obviously, the political leaders she hitched her star to were
nearly all losers on the national stage, and even at Georgetown,

where she was voted "best professor" four consecutive years, she still was denied tenure due to her lack of scholarly publications. But none of these disappointments could compare to the blow she had suffered in her personal life. With three daughters, two homes, three academic degrees, and a wealthy husband who doted on her, Madeleine was seemingly living the dream, or so she thought until 8 A.M. on January 13, 1982, when her husband without warning suddenly announced: he was in love with another woman, and their 22-year marriage was over. As he explained to Madeleine, he did still love her but in proportions that now fluctuated daily like the stock market, bobbing, according to his cold calculations, between 30 and 60 percent. Plus, he added with a twist of the knife—the other woman was younger and prettier.

Madeleine was floored. She was 44 years old and nearly alone— only her youngest daughter was still at home. "I had to put myself back together," she said, "and that was hard. It would have been easier if he had died. But I felt that I'd been betrayed." As painful as it was, this episode proved to be the turning point in her life. Awarded a lucrative divorce settlement, Madeleine could have quietly and comfortably whiled away her days, wallowed in grief, or grown bitter with anger and cynical with rage. These options would have been all too easy to grasp—and she rejected them all.

Instead, at this critical juncture in her life, during this period of great personal uncertainty and vulnerability, she turned to the one place where she could find an outlet for her anxieties, a channel for her energies, and a ballast that would not only stabilize her life as a newly single mother and career woman but also prepare her for navigating whatever adventures or adversities lay ahead, and that seminal place was *work*.

Work and career became her solace and salvation, and no job or position was too small or insignificant to offer an opportunity for personal and professional growth. As she later wrote,

> It didn't matter that [these stepping stones] had been placed at random and were sometimes slippery. I was determined not to fall in the river. . . . Slowly and steadily, as the 1980s progressed, I exchanged my feelings of loneliness for a sense of freedom. . . . . I learned to rely on myself [and soon] no longer felt like an egg without a shell. . . . There was so much new to explore and learn. I wanted to be ready, when the time came, to leap to the next stone.

The personal drive and determination that had long been channeled into her roles as dutiful housewife and loving mother now propelled her professional life, as Madeleine jumped at opportunities with a renewed passion and purpose. In addition to teaching at Georgetown, she accepted the presidency of a think tank (the Center for National Policy), served on the presidential campaigns mentioned above, and with the prominent connections she had made through her political activities she began hosting dinners at her home, where prominent Democrats discussed issues in foreign policy. These soirées put Madeleine on the D.C. map of movers and shakers, and it wasn't long before leaders from Congress, think tanks, law firms, and universities were scrambling for an invitation to Madeleine's Georgetown "salon."

"Opportunity," Thomas Edison reportedly said, "is missed by most people because it is dressed in overalls and looks like work." Determined to be the exception to Edison's famed rule, Madeleine positioned herself perfectly to take full advantage of the historic opportunities that came her way in the 1990s as a result of her tenacity and grit in the 1980s. She had received her breaks the old-fashioned way—she had *earned* them.

Although Madeleine, given her many years in the limelight of the international stage, would suffer her share of criticism and

U.S Secretary of State Madeleine Albright and others at the White House, briefing President Bill Clinton on the situation in Kosovo, March 31, 1999.

controversy alike, as nearly all do who serve in the public eye, the extraordinary course of her life—this rise to American prominence of a refugee from Europe who had survived the Holocaust, evaded the communists, and then broken the glass ceilings of the male-dominated corridors of Washington, D.C.—was an incredible tale, and it wasn't lost on the world. As Michael Shelden in the London *Telegraph* put it, "An obscure university lecturer at the time, she soon transformed herself into a leading authority on international diplomacy and—within a dozen years of her divorce—became the most powerful female official in American history." She could have also become the most powerful person in the Czech Republic. Václav Havel tried hard to convince Madeleine to succeed him as president of the country in 2003, but she rejected his supplications. She was flattered, of course, but her loyalties were now with her adopted country, the United States.

In 2012, Madeleine received America's highest civilian honor: the Presidential Medal of Freedom. During the award presentation, President Barack Obama related a story about Madeleine at a naturalization ceremony, when an Ethiopian man came up to her and said, "Only in America can a refugee meet the Secretary of State." To which Madeleine replied, "Only in America can a refugee *become* the Secretary of State."

Joe Louis

Born: May 13, 1914, LaFayette, Alabama
Died: April 12, 1981, Las Vegas, Nevada

CHAPTER 4

Battling Demons

Joe Louis

"Joe Louis was like the President of the United States," remarked his wife, and "how would you like to see the President of the United States washing dishes? That's how I felt about Joe wrestling." Louis, the famed "Brown Bomber" and former heavyweight boxing champion of the world, was a transcendent figure in American culture in the 1930s and 40s whose victories and defeats sent shock waves around the globe, even shaking the international political landscape. Songs were written about him, babies were named after him, and writers compared him to a new Moses who, with patience, purpose, and above all perseverance, could inspire "his people"—yes, African Americans, but also minorities the world over—to a new promised land of greater freedom and opportunity. As one of the some 40 songs written about him proclaimed, "He doesn't smile he doesn't frown / Just turns around and trucks on down." But due to a desperate need for money in the 1950s, with his boxing days well behind him, Louis had devolved into a circus side show of sorts on the professional wrestling circuit, and the result was embarrassing for all involved. It was like "Pavarotti singing in a striptease joint," wrote biographer Randy Roberts. Louis, on the other hand, defended his actions, including his later job as a greeter at Caesars Palace in Las Vegas, in his characteristically laconic way. Like a quick left jab, he'd snap: "Beats stealing."

As the longest-reigning heavyweight champion in boxing history (1937-49), Louis had made millions. But the more money he made, the more he spent, and the more he spent, the more he borrowed. And the entourage of freeloaders and hustlers who preyed on his kindness and ever-generous wallet grew ever larger. More damaging still were the federal taxes that had not been withheld from his prize money, and at a most inauspicious time—the tax levy on top earners had skyrocketed to *90 percent*. This left the fighter with more than a million-dollar debt (principal plus killer interest and penalties) to the Internal Revenue Service (IRS) by 1960; this debt would soar to some two million dollars by the time of his death two decades later. Clearly, Louis was the poster child for the fighter's paradox, delineated by sports writer John Lardner. "The rules of arithmetic do not apply to the fight business," he explained. "The longer you stay in it, the less you have."

Sex, drugs, and psychosis only added to Louis' troubles. Although soft-spoken and discreet, Louis enjoyed living large, and having grown up in poverty—the son of an Alabama sharecropper and the grandson of slaves—he found it hard to say no, to himself or to anyone. Whether it was a fine-looking suit or a fine-looking woman, the always dapper (and married) Louis couldn't settle for just one. He had extramarital affairs with many of the leading ladies of the day—including singer Lena Horne, actress Lana Turner, and figure skater Sonja Henie—and no number of diamonds, furs, and extravagant gewgaws that he showered his women with (he would be married four times) could eradicate their hurt and humiliation. Drugs entered the picture after a prostitute or a lover once shot him up with heroin while he slept. He welcomed the high—first from heroin and later cocaine—but like addicts everywhere, he discovered all too quickly that the escape from reality was all too fleeting, and never did it stem the barrage of phone calls, letters, lawyers, and threats issuing from the IRS. Psychosis then reared its ugly head, and when Louis' paranoid delusions finally got the better of him—he was building tents around his bed and taping up air conditioner units and heating vents to protect him from the gas he was certain was poisoning him—he was institutional-ized in 1970. Upon his release the following year, he returned to Vegas—the same, kind Joe whom everyone had loved but calmer and a bit slower due to medication.

Louis' life had taken a number of dark turns, but only a couple of times in his long career in the ring had he failed and fallen so far, embarrassing himself and his legions of fans. The last time—painful to watch but easy to understand—was on October 26, 1951, when he fought the young and hungry brawler Rocky Marciano. Slow, overweight, and with diminishing skills, Louis accepted the match and savage beating (he was knocked literally out of the ring in round eight) for one reason: for the guaranteed six-figure payday that he needed for the IRS. The earlier humiliation, on June 19, 1936, was harder to accept. Louis—as the number one heavyweight contender in the world, the most famous black man in the United States, and the embodiment of African American hopes and dreams during the Depression—was supposed to have won easily in this the final tune-up for his championship bout with James J. Braddock, the "Cinderella Man." But Louis, until that point undefeatable, did the unthinkable: he lost, and lost not just to anyone but to Max Schmeling—a white man, a German, the darling of Adolf Hitler, someone seen as a symbol of the Nazi regime. Louis' shocking loss by knockout in the 12th round stunned the 45,000 spectators in attendance at Yankee Stadium and millions of others, especially African Americans, who followed every jab and punch via radio. Poet Langston Hughes said he saw grown men weeping like children after the match. Lena Horne saw the loss through the lens of race: "[Louis] carried so many of our hopes. . . . But this night he was just another Negro getting beaten by a white man."

Louis understood better than anyone that the true foe that had beaten him was not Max Schmeling but the monsters in the mirror—his inflated ego, complacency, and overconfidence; his amazing talent was no match for their wily ways. Vowing never again to fall prey to these self-induced demons, Louis relit the passion within, trained harder than ever before, and dedicated his life to restoring his reputation and self-respect. "Guess I got a bit swell-headed, before and during the fight with Schmeling," said Louis, but "the swelling's gone down considerable now." And his single-minded mission of redemption paid off, when on June 22, 1937, he defeated Braddock and became the heavyweight champion of the world. But tainting the sweet taste of victory was the bitter tang of failure that still lingered from his loss to Schmeling, and only with a successful rematch with the German, set for one year later on June 22, 1938, could this vexing sense of incompleteness be finally slaked.

Many things had changed since Louis and Schmeling had met two year earlier. Louis' attitude, for one thing. But the world had changed, too—and not for the better. By the time of the rematch in June 1938 Hitler's bellicosity had crossed the Rubicon from mere rhetoric to reality. The Nazi leader had intervened in the Spanish Civil War, practicing large-scale aerial and armored assaults; signed military alliances with fascist Italy and Japan, foreshadowing the Axis alliance to come; and invaded and conquered Austria with impunity, absorbing the country into the German Reich. Tens of thousands of Jewish refugees were now streaming from the continent, the shattering glass of *Kristallnacht* was just four months away, and a full European war seemed inevitable to many. (Details of the *Kristallnacht* atrocities of November 9-10—the so-called "Night of Broken Glass" when Jewish businesses and synagogues were destroyed throughout Germany and some 30,000 Jewish men were arrested and sent to concentration camps—would soon be well known, but unreported until decades later was the courage of compassion afforded two teenage Jewish boys that harrowing night, when they were secreted to the safety of a hotel suite by the very hero of the regime perpetrating the atrocities. Their savior? Max Schmeling.)

So given the powder-keg state of world affairs, it was hardly
surprising that the long-awaited rematch between Schmeling and
Louis would be laced with portent and freighted with symbolic
meaning. Jesse Owens' performance at the Berlin Olympics in
1936 had been shadowed by many of these same political overtones,
but these shadows had darkened into full-blown storm clouds by
mid-1938. "The second Louis-Schmeling match connected dem-
ocratic America and fascist Germany in a compelling, dramatic
narrative," wrote Randy Roberts in *Joe Louis: Hard Times Man*; it
focused attention "on the differences between American and Nazi
ideologies, throwing anti-Semitism and racism into sharp relief."
The political ramifications of the contest were unmistakable, but
lest anyone miss the obvious, the *New York World-Telegram* christened the event "the Battle of Awesome Implications." But most
significantly for America in the long run, well beyond the immediate
scope of the Nazi threat and possibility of world war, was the fact
that the American at the helm of this symbolic war for democracy
was a *black* man—the first African American widely admired and
accepted by white America, the first black man to become a truly
national American hero. Or as comedian Dick Gregory would
wryly quip, Louis had become America's "Great White Hope."

Louis' fearlessness and tough, no-nonsense work ethic were just
what the country needed as the world teetered on the brink of war,
a point Franklin Roosevelt supposedly made explicit in a pre-bout
meeting with the boxer. "Joe, we need muscles like yours to beat
Germany," explained the president while dramatically squeezing
Louis' biceps. Although this widely-told tale is likely apocryphal
(Louis did meet Roosevelt but in 1935, and the president, in mid-

1938, would not have seen Germany as a certain wartime enemy and likely never would have said so publicly if he had), it reflects nonetheless the extraordinary symbolic import attached to the fight. Schmeling definitely did, however, hear from his country's leader. As he took center stage at Madison Square Garden for the official weigh-in on the afternoon of the fight, Schmeling was handed a cablegram. "To the next world's champion," it read. "Wishing you every success," signed Adolf Hitler.

Joe felt the pressure intensely—"The whole damned country was depending on me"—and he wasn't about to disappoint, not a second time. Before some 70,000 anxious fans at Yankee Stadium and another 100 million radio listeners worldwide—then the largest listening audience for any event in history—Louis took but a few seconds after the bout's opening bell to size up his opponent before unleashing a torrent of punches and punishment. With a flurry of jabs, hooks, one-twos, uppercuts, and a paralyzing kidney blow that elicited an audible cry of agony from Schmeling—like the scream of a tortured animal, said ringside spectators—Louis lashed out without mercy. Finding a visceral outlet for his two years of pent-up frustration, and amid cries from the crowd to "Kill that Nazi, kill him," Louis attacked with the swiftness of a Hitler blitzkrieg. Before the fight Louis had admitted, "I'm scared"—not scared that he would lose the fight but scared that he would literally kill Schmeling in the ring—and once the dazed and bloodied German had felt the canvas for a third time, the contest was over—in just 2 minutes and 4 seconds of the first round. "*Now* I feel like a champion," said Louis. African Americans nationwide felt like champions too, as did Jews around the world, who found in Louis and through his defeat of Schmeling hope that the Nazi menace would, in time, fall as well.

The aftermath of the fight was telling. Schmeling spent ten days in the hospital, recovering from broken vertebrae and even a hemorrhage, while Louis' heroic stature reached near mythical proportions. As David Margolick explained in *Beyond Glory: Joe Louis vs. Max Schmeling, and a World on the Brink* (2005),

> Louis was idolized as no one had ever been. . . . Black newspapers were filled with poems about him. Musicians composed songs about him. . . . [He and his

Popular World War II poster of Joe Louis, 1942.

accomplishments] let blacks everywhere think lofty and heretical thoughts; if he could shatter racial barriers, those barriers could not be so formidable. The sports pages put Louis' reach at seventy-six inches. In fact, it was global.

Global, indeed. Decades later a recording of Louis' victory over Schmeling would be played in a prison halfway around the world, inspiring another black leader and former boxer, one jailed for his own fight for social justice in a racially ravaged land—Nelson Mandela of South Africa. Years later, as a birthday present from President Bill Clinton, Mandela would receive an unused ticket to this seminal fight.

In the wake of his stunning victory, Louis accepted all challengers, successfully defending his heavyweight title 25 times, more than any other champion in any boxing division. After the country entered World War II in December 1941, Louis also did his civic duty. He volunteered for the army, giving up four years of lucrative paydays in the prime of his career, exchanging his $100,000 purses for the paltry pay of a soldier—$21 a month. But instead of fighting overseas Louis aided the country in a more useful way. He supported the war effort by touring military camps, visiting wounded soldiers, and participating in a grueling schedule of free exhibition matches for nearly two million soldiers across the United States, Europe, North Africa, and the Pacific. He fought two title defenses whose purses, amounting to more than $150,000, he donated to the Army and Navy relief societies (donations that the IRS would shockingly tax Louis on, and even levy interest on, later). He was said to have spent upwards of $250,000 of his own money as well on dinners and gifts for soldiers he met around the world during his four years of government service. This was precious money Louis didn't have, due to the paydays he had willingly forfeited during the war, and so he borrowed from his promoter, digging his ditch of debt even deeper. To make things worse, the IRS then rejected these expenses as job-related deductions, charging him years of interest and penalties on these wartime expenditures. (In the 1950s, when Louis accepted the embarrassing wrestling gigs in an effort to deal responsibly with his staggering debt, IRS agents would attend Louis' events, enjoy the show, and then collect the former champion's nightly pay from the box office. The IRS even took the trust funds that Louis had established for his children, and when his mother died and left him $600, the IRS took that as well.)

But despite the personal hardships his years of war service would cause him, Louis persevered and quietly pushed on, committed to helping the country any way he could. "We'll win because we're on God's side" was Louis' famed statement, widely publicized by the government on posters and in films and newsreels. As the ideal goodwill ambassador for race relations, Louis made countless public appearances to rally and recruit African Americans for the war effort. He appeared in morale-boosting films such as *This Is the Army* (1943) starring Ronald Reagan and *The Negro Soldier* (1944) produced by Frank Capra. Some blacks (including Muhammad Ali) would later brand Louis an Uncle Tom for his cooperation

"Everyone has a plan until they've been hit."

JOE LOUIS

with the U.S. government, which, in the eyes of many people then and today, had exploited Louis during the war years and then betrayed him afterwards with the viciousness with which the IRS hounded him. But Louis had a quick and clear answer for anyone who wondered why African Americans should bother to fight for the country abroad while racism and segregation continued at home and in the armed services as well: "There's nothing wrong with America that Hitler can fix."

Louis' years of selfless patriotism not only greatly aided the country at a time of dire need but helped to combat racism and weaken the color line throughout American life. He may not have led protests and sit-ins and demonstrations like those who followed decades later ("Some folks shout, some holler, some march and some don't," he said. "They do it their way; I do it mine"), but the absence of noise meant no absence of outrage and resistance. Louis understood the stark limitations of his day but still fought injustice whenever possible, and in his reserved but determined way, with grit and guts, he contributed to the civil rights movement to come. He insisted, for example, that ticket prices for his fights remain low so that his poorer black fans could afford to attend. When buses transporting soldiers to one of his exhibition matches were filled with nearly all white soldiers, and the few blacks onboard were forced to sit in the back, Louis refused to fight until the situation was remedied. In fact, Louis refused to fight before segregated crowds on American military bases and routinely sat on "white only" benches and used the "white only" pay phones, which on one army base even led to his arrest. Additionally, he used his power and prestige to help several blacks, most notably future baseball star and trailblazer Jackie Robinson, gain admission into officer candidate school during the war and then used this same political clout (not to mention bribes and expensive gifts) to save Robinson's military career. (Robinson had pummeled a trash-talking white officer on one occasion and, on another, been arrested and court-martialed for sitting next to light-skinned black woman whom the bus driver mistook as white). Without Louis' help, Robinson would likely never have been honorably discharged from the military, and without the honorable discharge Brooklyn Dodgers President Branch Rickey would have never chosen him to break the color bar in Major League Baseball, thereby denying him the opportunity to become the racial pioneer everyone knows him as today. A mere footnote in the annals of college sports and the Negro baseball leagues—this likely would have been Robinson's future without the generous aid of Joe Louis.

So it was largely with charm, not confrontation, that Louis exerted his greatest impact on the color barriers of his day. The multi-headed Hydra of fear and prejudice, hatred and intimidation, conflict and condescension, and misunderstanding and distrust that so often preyed on race relations of the time was often halted in its very tracks by Louis' mere presence, as even the most brick-hard of bigots could hardly ignore Louis' natural dignity and gentle, irenic nature. "There is no question," said an Army captain, "but that thousands of white soldiers drew a fairer and better evaluation of the negro soldier upon seeing and talking with Louis." Louis' effect on professional sports was especially evident. "If it wasn't for Joe Louis," admitted Jackie Robinson, "the color line in baseball would not have been broken for another ten years." Louis even helped to integrate professional golf, a sport he loved. When he received a sponsor's exemption to play in the 1952 San Diego Open, Louis became the first African American to play in a Professional Golf Association-sanctioned event.

Louis was frequently in his day called "a credit to his race," to which sportswriter Jimmy Cannon leveled the perfect response: "Joe Louis *is* a credit to his race—the *human* race."

When Louis died in 1981, a memorial service was held for him at Caesars Palace in Las Vegas, where his coffin was displayed inside a boxing ring. As the venue of so many boxing memories, this seemed only fitting. Just as appropriate was the eulogizer, someone named after two American heroes, Jesse Owens and Joe Louis. "Usually the champion rides on the shoulders of the nation and its people," said the Reverend *Jesse Louis* Jackson, "but in this case, the nation rode on the shoulders of its hero, Joe."

With a special dispensation from President Ronald Reagan, Louis was buried with full military honors at Arlington National Cemetery. One of the pallbearers at his funeral was an aging pugilist and former foe who had grown rich from his postwar work with the Coca-Cola company, who had come to Louis' aid in his times of financial need, and who reportedly even paid for a portion of Louis' funeral—Max Schmeling.

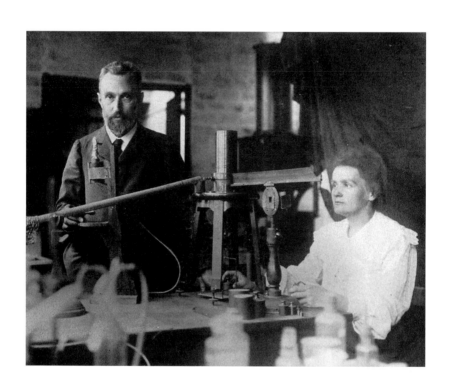

Marie Curie

Born: November 7, 1867, Warsaw, Poland
Died: July 4, 1934, near Sallanches, France

CHAPTER 5

Frail, Lonely, but Fearless

Marie Curie

S ex and scandal suddenly dominated their discussions when many of the world's most eminent scientists—including Albert Einstein, Max Planck, and Ernest Rutherford—gathered in Brussels in 1911 for the week-long Solvay Conference. They had convened to discuss the staggering impact of recent scientific discoveries—such as electrons, X-rays, nuclear radiation, and quantum theory—and it should have been the best of times for Marie Curie in particular, the sole woman in attendance. After all, while at the conference on November 4, she had received a telegram with magnificent news: she had just been awarded her *second* Nobel Prize, this time in chemistry for her discovery of radium and polonium (named by Marie in honor of her homeland), making her the first person to win the illustrious award more than once. But on the very same day of this wonderful announcement, as she crossed the lobby of her hotel on her way to a meeting, she was mobbed by reporters shouting: "How does it feel, Madame Curie, to be an adulteress, a homewrecker, a husband-stealer?"

Love and loneliness had led Marie to take a great risk with her career and reputation, and she was about to pay a heavy price for her recklessness. News of her affair with a brilliant and handsome (but married) young scientist at the conference, the splendidly mustachioed Paul Langevin, had hit the press. Langevin was her late husband's former student, a dear family friend, and a pioneer in the field of submarine sonar, and his estranged wife (the two were separated) had long threatened to expose her husband's relationship with the celebrity scientist. The wife had even accosted Marie on the street and threatened to kill her—a threat that was all too real, Paul warned Marie. And now she had exposed the couple in a very public way. She had hired someone to break into Paul's Paris apartment and to steal Marie's love letters to her husband. The letters were then given to the press, causing a feeding frenzy among the tabloid journalists of the day. "The fires of radium which so mysteriously warm everything around them, had a surprise in store for us," sniggered one paper. "They have just kindled a blaze in the hearts of the scientists who are studying their behavior with such tenacity—and the wife and children of one of these scientists are in tears."

Mocked as the "Vestal Virgin of Radium," Marie was suddenly the name on every tongue, the cynosure of every eye, and the object of endless scrutiny and editorial spleen. Some of the scallywags even suggested that her affair with Langevin had begun before her beloved husband (Pierre Curie, shown in the photograph with Marie at the start of this chapter) died, which was patently untrue, and that Pierre had not *accidentally* slipped in 1906 while crossing a rain-soaked street, where he was crushed and killed by a horse-drawn wagon, but had willingly lunged in front of the on-rushing beast in a fit of suicidal despair triggered by the shameless dalliance of his wife.

Langevin was spared much of the vitriol directed at Marie and weathered the scandal fairly well, as men of the day—such as Einstein, who had multiple extramarital affairs—tended to do. But then Langevin fanned the flames of the media firestorm even further when he challenged one of the journalists to a duel. After elaborate preparations, the two men met for the showdown but ultimately refused to fire their pistols. (A second duel was fought between the editors of rival papers covering the scandal, leaving one of the participants wounded by a sword.)

Mortified by the turn of events, Marie scarpered, leaving the conference and returning home to her two daughters in France. But escaping the maelstrom of controversy proved impossible. Upon arriving in France she found her home surrounded by a menacing crowd yelling insults at her and throwing rocks at her windows, causing Marie and her children to flee to a friend's house. "This illustrious woman had been reduced to wandering like a beast being tracked," said an observer quoted by Barbara Goldsmith in her fine biography of Curie.

Tracked, indeed.

The right-wing press had actually been hounding Marie for some time. Her misdeed? She had dared to apply for admission to France's preeminent scientific institution, an all-male bastion called the French Academy of Sciences. Her application spawned a cabal of conservatives, misogynists, xenophobes, and anti-Semites who conspired against her. Their assaults came fast and furious, as all aspects of her life were suddenly scrutinized and her reputation publicly besmirched. They oppugned the legitimacy of her appointment as the first female instructor at the University of Paris; they wondered aloud about her fitness as a mother, given her long hours in the lab; and they belittled her first Nobel Prize, hinting it was her husband, not she, who was the true genius in the family. She was branded a fraud and a charlatan who had ridden Curie's coattails to fame and fortune and was now trying to do the same via Langevin. The Swedish press in Stockholm, whence the Nobel Prizes are administered, attacked her looks, saying she had "a masculine face full of lines and looking much older than her forty-four years." Some papers even hired handwriting "experts" to study Marie's penmanship and phrenologists to comment on the shape of her head, all to glean insights into this now-tarnished character. Other journalists simply dismissed her as an alien Jew. (A foreigner she was; Jewish, she was not.)

The smear campaign worked—Marie failed to win admission to the academy. Nor did she get Langevin. He returned to his wife, took a new mistress, fathered a child with one of his students, and then, years later, brazenly asked Marie to give a lab position to his out-of-wedlock daughter—and she agreed. Although a union with Langevin was not to be for Marie, their lives would intersect in a special way years later, when Marie's granddaughter married Langevin's grandson.

Amid this year of turmoil, during which her male colleagues at the Sorbonne even pushed for her banishment from France, the young Einstein quickly came to her defense. "I am convinced that you [should] continue to hold this riffraff in contempt," he wrote to her, and "if the rabble continues to be occupied with you, simply stop reading that drivel. Leave it to the vipers it was fabricated for."

But the Nobel Prize committee was far less understanding. Even in 1903, when she and her husband shared the Nobel Prize for Physics with Henri Becquerel for their pioneering work on radioactivity (a term coined by Marie), the Nobel Committee had attempted to give the award only to the men, reflecting the dismissive way women scientists were commonly viewed at the time. *"They're too sentimental and emotional to conduct serious science"* was the feeling of the day; they may be worthy helpmates in the lab,

Marie Curie (seated second from right) at the Solvay Conference in Brussels, Belgium, 1911. Pictured behind her is Paul Langevin (far right), standing next to a young Albert Einstein.

but real science was the exclusive domain of the male. Accordingly, Pierre Curie was always referred to as "Doctor" or "Professor," but Marie—the two-time Nobel Prize winner—as merely "Madame Curie." But Pierre, to his credit, refused to accept the honor of the Nobel Prize unless Marie was duly included, and the Nobel authorities grudgingly agreed. Traveling to Stockholm to accept the prize, however, was then out of the question: Marie had suffered a miscarriage and was also mourning the death of her father. When they finally were able in 1905 to travel to Sweden to accept the prize, it was Pierre alone who delivered the acceptance speech—Marie was not even allowed on the stage and was relegated to listening to "their" acceptance speech with the audience. Given this context, it was hardly then surprising, in the wake of the embarrassing Langevin affair, that the Nobel Committee suggested that Marie not come to the public ceremony in Stockholm for her second Nobel Prize. But Marie refused to stay home. She proudly attended the ceremony, accepted her medal, and in a strongly worded speech took full credit for all of her accomplishments, past and present. She then returned to Paris, where she finally succumbed to the pressures, collapsed in exhaustion, and suffered a serious nervous breakdown and bout of depression.

Except for her years with her beloved husband and lab partner Pierre, which she called the "best and happiest" period of her life, Marie had encountered near constant struggle and adversity. Born Maria Skłodowska, she grew up under the yoke of the Russian

Empire, which then ruled Poland with an iron fist. Spies were everywhere, criticism of the government was illegal, and only Russian was permitted to be spoken. "Warsaw was then under Russian domination," wrote Marie, "and one of the worst aspects of this control was the oppression exerted on the school and the child." The schools "were watched by the police and overburdened with the necessity of teaching the Russian language even to children so young that they could scarcely speak their native Polish." The situation was especially hard on Marie, who, as the student savant of her school, was routinely singled out by Russian inspectors and grilled on her studies; these were terrifying and tense episodes that left Marie in tears. Her home life suffered as well, after the Russians stripped her father (a proud, Polish nationalist) of his teaching position, forcing the family to take in boarders to make ends meet. Young Marie lost her bedroom and had to sleep on the couch amid an increasingly crowded and chaotic household, and with the influx of boarders came an influx of disease. When Marie was six years old, both her sisters caught typhus from tenants—one sister recovered, but the older one died. Her mother would later succumb to tuberculosis. A tragic consequence of this period of contagion was her mother's decision to stop hugging, holding, or kissing her children, even banning them from sitting in her lap. The emotional isolation only confused the young Marie. Did her mother not love her? Had she done something wrong to warrant such rejection? This awful confluence of factors—the family instability, the snooping of Russian spies, the death of her sister, the death of her mother, and the family quarantine on affection—scarred Marie deeply, contributing to her adult insecurities, battles with

"Life is not easy for any of us. But what of that? We must have perseverance and, above all, confidence in ourselves. We must believe that we are gifted for something, and that this thing, at whatever cost, must be attained."

MARIE CURIE

depression, longings for love, woebegone look, and eventual austere and distant relationship with her own two daughters. Even Einstein, a dear friend who praised Marie "of all celebrated beings, the only one whom fame has not corrupted," admitted that, personally and emotionally, she was "cold as a herring."

When Marie finished her formal schooling at age 15—a time when women were banned from pursuing a college education in Poland—her father enrolled her in the "Floating University," which Polish teachers ran secretly at locales that changed regularly to escape the watchful eye of the Russians. It was here, in these clandestine classes, that Marie's serious but furtive interest in science began.

In fact, pursuing a career in science would never be easy for Marie. Even at age 24, after she had scraped together enough money to follow her sister to France to attend the University of Paris, her life remained hard. She could afford only a small, unheated attic apartment without running water, and it wasn't long before her poverty and malnutrition and long hours of study in the library, which at least was heated, got the better of her. Emaciated and fainting due to weakness, Marie was nursed back to health by her sister and brother-in-law.

But despite the many hardships and setbacks she faced, especially as a woman in a male-dominated field, Marie mustered the grit to persevere and push on, never giving in to adversity or allowing the exigencies of the moment to hinder her pursuit of the career to which she had dedicated her life. Her physical body, however, was less resilient than her spirit, and her years of exposure to radioactive elements and X-rays would eventually take their toll. (Her heavy exposure to the latter came during World War I, when she and her daughter Irène converted automobiles into mobile radiological units—nicknamed "little Curies"—and traveled to battlefield after battlefield to detect bullets, shrapnel, and broken bones in wounded soldiers, saving untold lives and restoring in the process her battered reputation in France.) Marie was still only in her thirties when her face wrinkled and her hair turned gray, making her look decades older than she was; more critically, she and Irène, as well as Irène's husband Frédéric, would all die from blood disorders (Marie from leukemia or aplastic anemia) or organ failures believed to have been caused by their extended exposure to these dangerous substances. At a time when the health hazards of radiation were not properly understood, Marie had carried radioactive material in her coat and stored it in her desk. She even noted how much she enjoyed gazing at "the lovely sight" of the "glowing tubes" of radioactive material in her lab at night. To this day, Marie's papers and belongings remain so radioactive that scholars and researchers can only handle them with protective clothing and after agreeing to a waiver of liability.

Notable awards would follow for Marie and her remarkable family. Irène and her husband Frédéric, like Marie and Pierre before them, also won a joint Nobel Prize, the 1935 chemistry prize for their discovery of *artificial* radioactivity, and Marie's other daughter Ève—a writer and concert pianist widely hailed as one of the most beautiful women in Paris in the 1920s and 30s—wrote the 1937 biography of her mother that won the American National Book Award for nonfiction and inspired the 1943 Hollywood film *Madame Curie* starring Greer Garson as Marie and Walter Pidgeon as Pierre. Ève's husband, Henry Labouisse, the American ambassador to Greece, was also executive director of UNICEF when the agency won the Nobel Prize for Peace in 1965, making him the fifth member of the Curie family to receive a Nobel Prize. An additional honor for Marie followed 30 years later, in 1995, when her ashes were enshrined in the famed Panthéon in Paris, making her the first woman to receive this honor on the basis of her own achievements.

When Pierre gave the Nobel acceptance speech in 1905, he made clear his belief, held by Marie as well, that "mankind will derive more good than harm from the new discoveries," such as the ones they had made in the field of radiation. But in an eerie twist of fate, on the very day of Marie's death on July 4, 1934, a little-known physicist from Hungary named Leo Szilard registered a patent for a device that could produce a nuclear chain reaction of extraordinary power, paving the way 11 years later for that ultimate weapon of mass destruction: the lethally radioactive atomic bomb.

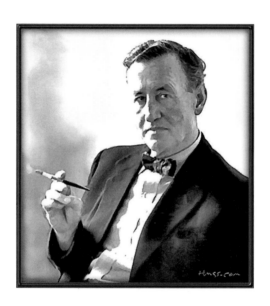

Ian Fleming

Born: May 28, 1908, London, England
Died: August 12, 1964, Canterbury, England

CHAPTER 6

Stumbling With No Loss of Enthusiasm

Ian Fleming

In the weeks and months after John Kennedy took office in January 1961, the world and the world's media couldn't get enough of the dynamic new king and queen of America's "Camelot." From what John and Jackie wore to what John and Jackie ate, the world wanted to know—including what the dazzling new American president *read.* When Kennedy, in a March 1961 article in *Life* magazine, listed among his ten favorite books Ian Fleming's *From Russia, With Love,* the fifth of Fleming's James Bond novels, the effect of the endorsement was stunning and swift: Fleming suddenly became the best-selling spy novelist in the world, selling millions of copies of his books and spawning the phenomenal film franchise that continues to this day.

Such success was wildly out of character for Fleming, who was long the black sheep of his wealthy, distinguished family. Robert Fleming, his grandfather, was one of the shrewdest and most successful Scottish financiers of his day, and Ian's father, Valentine, was a barrister and MP (Member of Parliament) and the quintessential English gentleman, educated at Eton and Oxford and noted for doing "everything just right." When "Val" was killed by a shell on the Western Front of World War I on May 20, 1917, just before Ian's ninth birthday, the obituary in *The Times* of London was written by one of Val's dear friends—Winston Churchill. Ian's father may have died, but his spirit would live on. A copy of the obituary, signed by Churchill, would hang in Ian's home for the rest of his life, and the memory of this brave and manly man, wielded like a weapon of intimidation by Ian's mother as biographer Andrew Lycett notes, would help inspire that most manly of literary creations—James Bond. Peter, Ian's older brother, followed in his father's very respectable footsteps: he graduated from both Eton and Oxford, married Oscar-nominated actress Celia Johnson, became a celebrated writer and adventurer, and assisted overseas with intelligence operations during World War II, for which he was richly praised and decorated.

Ian took a less impressive path. He, too, attended Eton, but he could never match the academic brilliance of his brother, and the contrast between the boys could not have been starker. "Peter was the sort of thoroughbred who comes out of the stable glossy, confident, superior to all the other horses, a natural winner," noted one observer. "Whereas Ian had been the sort of horse that arrives sweating and nervous at the starting post, more likely to throw its rider than win its race." In fact, Ian exhibited such a lackluster interest in everything but athletics that his mother removed him from school (and the ever-broadening shadow of his brother) in 1926 and sent him to the Royal Military College at Sandhurst. Ian took to soldiering, however, no more readily than he had taken to academics, though he did excel at one extracurricular activity that Bond would also master: womanizing. With charm, good looks, affluence, and now a dashing uniform to boot, Ian had an easy way with the ladies, who called him "Glamour Boy"—so easy, in fact, that he soon contracted gonorrhea. His mother was mortified as well as incensed, especially since she had tapped her royal contacts—Ian's grandmother was close to Queen Mary—to get Ian a commission with a choice regiment. So she pulled him out of Sandhurst in 1927 (due to "sickness") and sent him to the continent, where he perfected his linguistic skills in German and French at schools in Austria, Germany, and Switzerland, all in preparation for the Foreign Office exam and a diplomatic career. Ian took the exam, and he passed—but with a score so low that a diplomatic post was never a possibility. Once again his mother intervened, pulling still more strings to get him a position with the Reuters news agency—a position Fleming loved and for which he traveled to Moscow, a city then teeming with spies and secret agents, in 1933 to cover one of Stalin's notorious "show trials." The experience gave Fleming a first-hand look at Soviet communism, the backdrop of his Cold War-era capers to come. He even brashly wrote to Stalin and asked him for an interview, to which the Soviet leader replied with a personally signed letter, declining the offer. Fleming then bowed to family wishes and the pressure to earn serious money and entered the realm of banking and investment, becoming, in the words of a colleague, "among the world's worst" stockbrokers.

So as Fleming turned 30, a time when most men were busily entrenched in or carving out their life's calling, his résumé read like a college guide to careers. Student, soldier, diplomat, journalist, banker, stockbroker, investor—he had dabbled in each, failed at most, and was still floundering to find his special niche.

It was then, at this critical time in Fleming's life, that World War II intervened and offered him something new and substantial, even life-changing in the long run: he became an assistant to the director of British naval intelligence, Rear Admiral John Godfrey, the model for Bond's boss "M." In a word, Fleming became a *spymaster.* Although few had high hopes for Ian in this latest endeavor, Commander Fleming actually flourished, exhibiting a passion for intelligence planning and detailed administrative work. He even traveled to Washington, D.C., to help organize the Office of the Coordinator of Information, a precursor to the Office of Strategic Services and the CIA, and he was the mastermind of assorted secret

Actor Sean Connery (left) with Ian Fleming on the set of *Dr. No* (1962), the first James Bond film.

missions and acts of sabotage. He especially enjoyed the gadgets associated with spying, such as hidden cameras, invisible ink, and gas pistols disguised as fountain pens. Such gadgetry would become a mainstay of the Bond arsenal.

Fleming was certainly, during his wartime years in covert operations, more brain than brawn, more Sherlock than Bond, more of an arm-chair paper-pusher and a dreamer of plots than a dagger-wielding Rambo red in tooth and claw, but to a desk he was never chained for long, and danger and derring-do still managed to find him. For example, when he flew to Paris on June 13, 1940, it was only one day before German troops marched into the city. With the enemy just hours away, Fleming raided the safe at the Rolls-Royce office in Paris where British intelligence stashed its funds and then escaped to Bordeaux, some 300 miles southwest near the Atlantic coast. But with the Germans pushing southward in hot pursuit, Fleming once again had to act swiftly. He destroyed sensitive documents at the local British consulate, and with the money he had seized in Paris, he began bribing local merchant sailors and car ferry pilots (and threatening those he couldn't bribe) into sailing refugees, many of them Jewish, to safety in England. Fleming then fled France and, after stops in Spain and Portugal, returned to London, arriving just in time for the relentless German bombardment known as the Blitz (September 1940-May 1941). On three occasions he narrowly escaped with his life, when structures he was occupying were struck and reduced to rubble.

His intelligence activities included "Operation Goldeneye," a plan to preserve communications with the strategic Allied stronghold of Gibraltar, and even to conduct sabotage operations there, should

Spain ally itself with or fall to the Axis powers; and an extraordinary espionage mission called "Operation Mincemeat," a campaign to misdirect German attention to Greece and Sardinia while the Allies were planning their July 1943 invasion of Sicily—the largest amphibious landing up to that time. "Operation Mincemeat," in fact, was one of the war's most successful deception operations. Both ingenious and outrageous, it was akin to the barely credible escapades soon to be associated with James Bond. "The business of deception, handling double agents, deliberate leakages and building up in the minds of the enemy confidence in a double agent, needed the sort of corkscrew mind which I did not possess," admitted Godfrey, but his assistant, Fleming, possessed such thoughts in volumes, and "Operation Mincemeat" stemmed from one of the 51 suggestions for counterintelligence operations set forth by Fleming under Godfrey's name in a famous intelligence report issued just three weeks into the war in late September 1939 called the "Trout Memo," which compared good counterintelligence activities to the patience and deception of an expert trout fisherman. "At first sight, many of [Fleming's wartime schemes] appear somewhat fantastic," said Godfrey, "but nevertheless they contain germs of some good ideas; and the more you examine them, the less fantastic they seem to appear."

In this case of "Operation Mincemeat," drama was mixed with a heavy dash of theatrics. The mission entailed creating a false identity for a dead man whose body would be staged for the enemy to find—an idea that Fleming, ever the bibliophile, took from a 1937 detective novel (*The Milliner's Hat Mystery*) by World War I spy-catcher-turned-novelist Basil Thomson. Specifically, the Mincemeat mission involved dressing the corpse of a London vagrant (who had killed himself by swallowing rat poison) as a British serviceman, planting bogus invasion plans in his uniform, and then floating the body off the coast of Spain where German agents were sure to find it. The scheme worked perfectly, whereupon a memo was sent to Churchill: "Mincemeat swallowed rod, line and sinker."

More famous still is Fleming's involvement in creating the intelligence-gathering commando group called the 30 Assault Unit (30AU). Its purpose was to move into enemy territory ahead of advancing Allied troops in the hope of capturing enemy documents, equipment, and even personnel. Among their captured booty were torpedoes, land mines, top secret documents, and even a one-man submarine whose commander, long dead and decomposing, was still upright and eerily peering through the periscope. The unit was trained in assorted Bond-like activities, such as hand-to-hand combat and even safecracking, and it eventually comprised more than 300 men—"Red Indians," as Fleming termed the "tough commando types," and a group of Royal Marines who provided them with cover. The unit's baptism by fire, however, was calamitous. It was part of the disastrous raid on Dieppe, the German-held port on the northern coast of France, on August 19, 1942, when Canadian forces stormed the beaches and were mowed down by German guns; thousands of Canadians were killed, wounded, or captured that dreadful day. The unit's reported aim was the capture of one of Germany's new four-rotor Enigma encoding machines. But no such capture was possible amid the bloody melee. Ian had requested permission to go ashore with his unit, but his request had been swiftly denied—he was considered too valuable an asset to put in harm's way and privy to too much secret information should he be captured. But danger still found him, as the ship he stayed on during the raid, some 800 yards off the beachfront, was hit by enemy fire that killed one serviceman and injured several others.

A later success for 30AU occurred shortly before the end of the war in Europe in 1945, when the massive archives of the German navy going back to the Franco-Prussian War of 1870-71 were captured, along with the German officers in charge of them. Amid the haste to wrap up the intelligence operation, and to relocate the historical material back to England, keeping it out of Russian hands (Soviet troops were fast approaching), Fleming reportedly ordered the "elimination" of the two German officers. When his young lieutenant refused to kill the prisoners of war, Fleming rescinded the order.

World War II had clearly been the seminal experience of Fleming's life, as it was for most men of his day. He had persevered through the many missteps and misadventures of his yeasty youth and grown and matured, finding in the process, in the words of biographer Ben Macintyre, "a world of secret agents and espionage, of adventure, violence and intrigue, that delighted him, satisfying both his intellect and romanticism." But the war years were heart-wrenching ones as well: his younger brother Michael had been wounded and captured in Normandy in late May 1940, during the frantic retreat of British troops to Dunkirk. He died from his wounds, while in captivity, on October 1.

Coming down from the high of the excitement and intrigue of the war years would not be easy for the ever-restless Fleming, and

"Never say 'no' to adventures. Always say 'yes,' otherwise you'll lead a very dull life."

IAN FLEMING

he thought long and hard about how to escape what he considered the most abhorrent of fates: the tedium of ordinary, everyday life. So after great contemplation, he settled on a career that would offer him both income and access to the exotic: he would manage the foreign correspondents for the Kemsley chain of newspapers, which included the *Sunday Times.* The post provided sufficient money for his expensive sports cars and bespoke wardrobe and, most importantly, allowed him ample time to winter at his home in Jamaica, which he christened "Goldeneye." It was there in 1952, in a matter of weeks (some say eight, others say a mere four), that he wrote his first Bond novel, *Casino Royale*, the manuscript for which he fine-tuned with his latest toy, an expensive talisman of sorts of what he hoped was his future success as a writer—a gold-plated typewriter. The novel, inspired by a visit to a casino in Portugal during the war, was published in April 1953 and was indeed an instant success.

Fleming named his debonair secret agent with the license to kill after a most unlikely source: American ornithologist James Bond. Fleming was an avid birder, and his "Jamaican bible," his *vade mecum,* was Bond's *Field Guide of Birds of the West Indies.* "It struck me," said Fleming, "that this brief, unromantic, Anglo-Saxon and yet very masculine name was just what I needed, and so a second James Bond was born." In exchange for using Bond's name, wrote Fleming years later in a letter to the ornithologist's wife, "I can only offer you or James Bond unlimited use of the name Ian Fleming for any purposes you may think fit. Perhaps one day your husband will discover a particularly horrible species of bird which he would like to christen in an insulting fashion by calling it Ian Fleming."

Fleming modeled the Bond novels on the many spymasters and missions he had dealt with during the war, but 007's signature characteristics were based heavily on Fleming's own complex personality. As recounted by biographer Lycett, these included his fondness for smoking and drinking (Fleming was consuming 70 custom-made cigarettes and a bottle of gin daily at age 38), his love of card games, fast cars, and outdoor activities (such as golfing, skiing, mountain-climbing, spelunking, shark-hunting, treasure-hunting, snorkeling, and diving), and even his affection for sex. Fleming's obsession with overindulgence led to a serious heart attack in 1961. He died three years later, having written 12 Bond novels, two short-story collections featuring Bond, as well as the popular children's story *Chitty Chitty Bang Bang*.

In the end, there was one salient constant in Fleming's rich and varied life: although he had flitted and floated from career to career, seldom succeeding at any endeavor before the war, he never allowed his serial failures to extinguish his ambitions, his thirst for adventure, his drive to escape the trammels of his overbearing mother and the enormous shadow of his idealized father, or his will to live his life on his own terms. He was the living embodiment of that oft-cited definition of success, frequently attributed to Winston Churchill—"stumbling from failure to failure with no loss of enthusiasm"—and it was this persistent, even aggressive sense of wonder, undampened by defeat, and boyish passion for new experiences, either real or through the artifice of fiction and fantasy, that eventually steered him to the career that cemented his destiny and spurred his creation of one of the most famous and enduring characters in literature and film.

Thomas Edison

Born: February 11, 1847, Milan, Ohio
Died: October 18, 1931, West Orange, New Jersey

CHAPTER 7

Failure and Perspiration

Thomas Edison

While working on his signature invention, the light bulb, Thomas Edison and his assistants tested more than 6,000 plants for material suitable to use as the filament. Such tedious and exhausting work—in this case, one of the most laborious efforts in the annals of experimentation—resulted in Edison's greatest invention, and greatest maxim: "Genius is one percent inspiration and 99 percent perspiration."

Homeschooled by his mother and then largely self-taught, Edison was the quintessential workaholic and the epitome of Yankee ingenuity. He was called the "Wizard of Menlo Park," a community in New Jersey where he lived and worked and which today lies within the township of Edison. His various inventions—including the first reliable and commercially viable electric light bulb, the electrification and lighting of cities via a central power station, the carbon microphone that made early telephones clearly audible, his pioneering commercial film studio, the first industrial research and development laboratory, and (Edison's favorite) the phonograph—revolutionized daily life and profoundly affected cultural history. He was the man, concluded historian Richard Norton Smith, who had done what no mortal could seemingly do: he had "banished the darkness." A folk hero of the modern, industrial age, Edison was the most recognized American in the world between 1879, when he designed his famed light bulb, and his death in 1931. It is fitting that the graphic symbol of ingenuity and a "bright idea," one recognized the world over, is the simple sinuous shape of Edison's iconic light bulb.

Edison's extraordinary work ethic required great grit, which was the same patience and perseverance required to survive a most unforgiving time in history, when there was little tolerance of hands-on learners like Thomas. To say that Edison was inquisitive as a child would be a grave understatement, for he was arguably curious to a fault. He peppered adults with question after question, and when he didn't get the immediate answers he sought, he set off to find them by trial and error himself, dangers be damned. He was so energetically impatient that in his teenage years he even developed the habit of writing entirely without punctuation, as if commas and periods were personal assaults on his ambition. He also disdained sleep—beyond the three to four hours he indulged in nightly—as a wasteful "heritage from our cave days," opting instead for strategic power naps, at any time and any place. This restless individualism was ingrained in the Edison clan—Thomas's great-grandfather was exiled to Canada from New Jersey due to his royalist allegiance during the American Revolution, and Thomas's father was then exiled back to the United States from colonial Canada for his *anti*-royalist rabblerousing in the 1830s. A similar spirit made young Thomas a classroom troublemaker, in constant rebellion against the rote-based, straitjacket teaching methods of the day that allowed little wiggle room for tactile, hyperactive, and heuristic learners like Thomas. (This explains the adult Edison's great fondness for Italian educator Maria Montessori and her freedom-based, discovery-oriented approach to education.) And when his teachers reportedly branded him "addled" and hinted he was perhaps even learning challenged, suffering from what biographer Neil Baldwin has likened to attention deficit disorder, young Thomas merely doubled his resolve never to return to the classroom. This left his mother, a teacher fortunately blessed with the patience of Job, with little choice but to begin a regimen of homeschooling. Her devotion to her son and his education only deepened Thomas's love for his mother and for learning itself.

His father, on the other hand, was far less tolerant. He found his son strange and vexing, or as Thomas would later say, "My father thought I was stupid, and I almost decided I must be a dunce." His father would squinny with suspicion at his often sickly son who didn't care to play games or go fishing with the other boys, preferring instead to read or to experiment in solitude with chemicals or electricity. Although his father influenced Thomas's intellectual development by introducing him to the ideas of political philosophers such as Thomas Paine, he exhibited little patience with or sympathy for Thomas when the latter (usually called Al or Alva), age three or four, disappeared for hours on end one day, only to be found sitting atop a nest of goose and chicken eggs, trying to hatch them; or when, at age six, Alva burned down the family barn (and nearly the town as well) due to his fascination with fire and its movement; or when Alva was clawed by two cats whose fur he was rubbing furiously together in an attempt to produce static electricity; or when young Thomas convinced a rather dimwitted playmate to ingest a near-lethal dose of effervescent powders in order to see if the resulting gases building in his chum's stomach could engender human flight. His father's reaction in such cases (a reaction hardly uncommon for those times) was not patience, understanding, or a good, stern lecture but rather a reach for the switch, and frequent whippings at home—and at school as well by his impatient teachers—were young Edison's reward for his innate inquisitiveness. In fact, in the wake of the notorious barn-burning incident, the punishment took the form of a *public* whipping, which his father conducted in the town square for all to see. As Edison biographer Matthew Josephson noted, "It was like a scene out of the time of the Puritans in New England."

Such earnestness may have resulted in mayhem and lashings for young Thomas, but it was the key to his adult accomplishments. Yet, for every success that Edison experienced—he held 1,093 U.S. patents—there were exponentially more failures and disappointments. Take, for instance, his first patented invention, created in 1869 when he was just 22: the electrographic vote recorder. Designed for use by legislative bodies such as the U.S. Congress, it offered a way to record and tally the number of yeas and nays in voting, but legislators proved little inclined toward contraptions that expedited voting and left less time for political horse-trading. The invention flopped. Edison's electric pen also struggled to take off. Patented in 1876, it was a mechanical, portable document copier that some have called the first electric appliance sold in the United States. The pen had a needle-tipped rod that went up and down like a mini-jackhammer, perforating the paper as the person wrote. The result was a stencil that could then be placed on a portable press with an ink roller, which came along with the pen. Any product like this that could improve the efficiencies of administrative tasks in the budding new commercial enterprises of the day had great potential. But Edison's pen was heavy and noisy and contained a cumbersome battery, and after a brief period of success spurred by its novelty, the product faded in the face of better products. Its influence, however, didn't end there. His pen inspired not only the

Henry Ford speaking into the ear of Thomas Edison, likely because of the latter's deafness, *c.* 1930.

duplication process that would takes its place, the mimeograph (1887), but also the first electric tattoo machine. The latter, patented in 1891, was to a large extent Edison's pen with additional needles and an ink reservoir. So Edison's sci-tech failure would foster a genre of art: "body art," that is.

Edison's "talking doll," which had a crank in its back where later incarnations would have a string to pull, was another idea ahead of its time—it's been called the first audio-recorded product ever produced for entertainment—but a failure in its day. Released in 1890, Edison sunk thousands of dollars into this venture, hoping to capitalize on the doll craze of the Victorian era. He even planned a 15,000-square-foot factory in Antwerp, Belgium, to be run by "cheap labor," to manufacture the toy for the European market. And the prospects seemed very good: he was flooded with advance orders for the doll. But once distributed, the toys were returned as quickly as they went out. Their delicate mechanisms could not withstand shipping and even moderate handling, especially by a child, meaning the dolls, in most instances, swiftly went mute. The toys were also so expensive to produce that their selling price (the equivalent of more than $200 today) was prohibitive. Once again Edison was ahead of his day in identifying a market opportunity, but the manufacturing methods then available couldn't yet deliver a practical product. (In 2015, new technology enabled the public to hear, for the first time in many years, Edison's dolls "speak," and the recordings—made by adult women (called the first recording artists) screeching out bedtime stories and prayers in a childish voice—are frightening, more likely to spur nightmares than tender thoughts in little girls. In fact, Edison later called the crude and creepy dolls his "little monsters.") The venture was a costly failure.

Edison also failed in some very public endeavors. He spent more than ten years trying to efficiently extract iron from beach sand and low-grade ore, and though his decade of attempts led to numerous patents and novel production methods that were applied in other businesses—for example, his rock-crushing technology revolutionized the production of Portland cement and concrete— his venture amounted to an abject failure that left him bankrupt; called "Edison's Folly," it is frequently cited as the biggest failure of his life. He spent another decade producing and marketing, and then redesigning and remarketing, numerous batteries for the electric car, which dominated the early automotive industry in the late 19th century. But his batteries were plagued with one problem after another, and during the decade he spent retooling his product, his dear friend and protégé Henry Ford revolution-ized transportation with his *gasoline*-powered Model T. (Ford would later receive the cherished gift of Edison's "final breath," supposedly captured by Thomas's son in a sealed test tube, that is now on display at the Henry Ford Museum in Dearborn, Michi-gan.) Another very public failure occurred during the "War of the Currents," in which his direct current (DC) mode of transmitting electricity, which had difficulties carrying charges long distances, lost out to the now-standard alternating current (AC) method of Nikola Tesla and George Westinghouse.

But defeats like these, as disappointing as they were, never de-feated Edison—that is, they never demoralized him to the point of destroying his drive, initiative, and ambition. To him, the half-filled cup was never half-empty, as he could forever find (to change

"I have not failed.
I've just found 10,000
ways that won't work."

THOMAS EDISON

the metaphor) that inspiring ray of light amid the darkest clouds of failure. For with unwavering grit and faith in his own abilities, he had the extraordinary power to leave failure behind him and to push on with confidence and earnest industry to new endeavors. "Where others might see disaster and failure," noted Edison biographer Paul Israel, "he was always optimistically looking for opportunities and seeing the possibility of new directions for improvements." This resilience was never more evident than in the wake of the iron ore fiasco. "I have never felt better in my life," he said about his years living in Spartan surroundings amid the miners and mammoth steam shovels, which he'd watch with the wide-eyed fascination of a child. "Hard work, nothing to divert my thoughts, clear air, simple food made life very pleasant." When reminded that the General Electric stock that he had sold to fund the failure would now be worth many millions of dollars, he replied with a *c'est la vie* shrug of insouciance: "It's all gone, but we had a hell of a good time spending it."

Years later, in 1914, when a horrific explosion and fire at his New Jersey factory destroyed ten buildings, along with tons of equipment and priceless records and prototypes, Edison refused once again to shake his fist at the gods of misfortune or to feel sorry for himself. Instead, he quickly, well-nigh immediately, accepted the reality of the situation he could not change and focused on the one element he could always influence, as we all can, if we only try: the future. But the future, for Edison, could wait for at least one night, for there was a mesmerizing scene before him that he wanted no one to miss. "Go get your mother and all her friends," he told his son Charles. "They'll never see a fire like this again." When interviewed by the *New York Times* about the devastating conflagration that had reduced to ashes his assets worth $1 million dollars (the equivalent of some $23 million today), Edison continued to look forward, not backward. "Although I am over 67 years old, I'll start all over again tomorrow." And so he did, for to Edison, there was always a tomorrow, a tomorrow of possibilities and endless opportunities.

But if vast material loss and staggering business failures were no match for Edison's irrepressible grit, what about his damnable physical affliction, the one that had bedeviled him since childhood and that would have defeated and demoralized many a lesser man—his deafness? Could grit conquer even this?

Hearing loss ran in his family, and by his early teens Thomas was likely technically deaf. What exactly caused the hearing loss has long been debated, and Edison himself gave various explanations. Scarlet fever, untreated ear infections as a child, and a family disposition towards middle-ear ailments were doubtless factors, though the more legendary explanation is the "ear-boxing" incident. According to lore, Edison, then age 12 or 13, was working as a newsboy and "candy butcher" (concessionaire) on the Grand Trunk Railroad running between Detroit and Port Huron, Michigan, where his family then lived, selling newspapers and treats to the passengers while, during his off hours, conducting experiments in a makeshift lab he had built in the baggage car. When a sudden lurch of the train led to the toppling of some phosphorus and a fire in his lab, the outraged conductor severely boxed Thomas's ears—spurring the deafness—and threw him off the train. This story is full of the pathos and drama commonly found in Horatio Alger tales of uplift. But it wasn't true. Years later Edison corrected the story. It seems, while running late for work one day, he had tried unsuccessfully, while laden with his heavy newspapers, to jump aboard the moving locomotive. The conductor reached out to help him, lifting him by his ears and hauling him onboard, inadvertently causing something to "snap inside my head," said Edison. After that, he could only hear "a few words now and then," until he "settled down to a steady deafness."

But whatever the actual causes of the hearing loss, Edison refused to see his disability as a disadvantage. In fact, like many successful people and high achievers, he refused to see his misfortune as anything but a blessing in disguise and a source of inspiration, a special gift through which "in my isolation . . . I had time to think things out." As with the other greats of grit highlighted in these pages, Edison rejected a life of self-pity and excuse-making and opted instead to fight on in the face of adversity and loss, and by channeling misfortune into motivation, he transformed a serious life-inhibiting liability—one of the most limiting of all physical afflictions—into a life-enriching asset.

Nevertheless, watching Edison deal with his disability was heartbreaking at times. On one occasion, during a visit to Edison's home, Maria Montessori was brought to tears while watching the aging inventor lean over and bite the side of his piano, clamping down on it with his teeth in the hope of "hearing" the music vibrate through his mouth. Considering Edison's invention of the phonograph, the tragic irony of the situation was not lost on anyone.

Walt Disney

Born: December 5, 1901, Chicago, Illinois
Died: December 15, 1966, Los Angeles, California

CHAPTER 8

Adversity as Teacher

Walt Disney

"Johnnie, get your gun,
Get your gun, get your gun . . .
Pack your little kit,
Show your grit, do your bit . . ."

George M. Cohan's hit song *Over There* (1917) inspired countless young men to do their bit and show their grit during World War I. Among the thousands who answered the call to service were those training as Red Cross ambulance drivers at a base in South Beach, Connecticut. On the face of it, there was nothing particularly special about this Red Cross unit. After all, by the time 50 of the young men had crossed the mine-laden Atlantic on a converted cattle ship called the *SS Vaubin* and finally reached their destination (Le Havre, France), it was December 4, 1918—the war had ended three weeks earlier. But amid this long-forgotten unit of volunteers were two visionaries whose future empires would forever change modern culture, commerce, and daily life: a 16-year-old Walt Disney and a 15-year-old Ray Kroc, the future founder of McDonald's. Both boys had quit school and lied about their ages in order to join the war effort. Disney, however, was part of the unit of drivers that shipped to France; Kroc was not selected for service overseas and was sent home. Although the boys obviously knew one another as part of the same unit, they did not become friends. In fact, Kroc and the other drivers considered "Diz," as Disney was called, a rather "strange duck." It seems, while Kroc and the other guys enjoyed skirt-chasing in town during their free time, Disney preferred to stay behind on the training base—to draw . . . to draw cartoons, no less.

Although trained as an ambulance driver, Disney actually spent little time overseas transporting the sick and the wounded. Driving, however, still dominated his days: he became a chauffeur and tour guide for high-ranking officials and their families. One of the highlights for Disney was when he tooled around the French countryside with the ten-year-old son of General "Black Jack" Pershing, commander of the American forces in France. Disney also had time to sharpen his skills as an artist. He drew cartoon characters on the canteen menus and on the canvas sides of his ambulances, and he even submitted drawings to the leading magazines of the day—all of his work was rejected. But if his time in France fell short of the heroic adventure he had dreamed of when he volunteered a year before, his "wartime" experience was hardly for naught. For Disney viewed every situation as an opportunity in disguise, and this chapter in his life was no different. "The things I did during those ten months I was overseas added up to a lifetime of experience . . . I know being on my own at an early age . . . made me more self-reliant."

Upon returning in the fall of 1919 to his family's home in Kansas City, Walt announced his intent to commit his life to art. His father—a short, skinny, splenetic taskmaster who struggled financially, uprooted the family often, and, like Thomas Edison's father, often beat his sons (with the side of a saw and the handle of a hammer)—was both dumbfounded and incensed by his son's intentions. "He never understood me," said Walt. "He thought I was a black sheep. This nonsense of drawing pictures!" But with unshakeable determination and infectious exuberance (and perhaps galvanized by a desire to be everything his father wasn't), the self-motivated and largely self-taught Walt was hell-bent on fashioning a career from his endless scribblings.

And an art position he landed rather quickly. He received an apprenticeship at a local commercial art shop, where he illustrated advertisements and catalogs for farm equipment and department stores. Though his duties called for little creativity, Walt was ecstatic—he was only 17 years old and working as a professional artist! But the joy was fleeting, for the end of the Christmas catalog season brought an end to his job. It was then, while Walt was scouring for work as a newspaper cartoonist, that an unexpected figure re-entered his life and changed its course both personally and professionally: fellow high school dropout Ub Iwerks, who had also been laid off from the local commercial art shop, reached out to him. Ub was depressed and down on his luck, desperate for money to support his mother, and he needed help. From Walt's perspective, the answer to both of their problems was right before them: they would pool their complementary talents and personalities and go into business together. After all, where Ub was shy, Walt was bold, and while Ub, a superb artist and creative mind, could prolifically produce the requisite artwork (Iwerks would later receive an Academy Award nomination for the special effects he created for Alfred Hitchcock's *The Birds*), Walt could serve as the grand visionary who would develop the business opportunities that would make their career dreams come true. So in 1920, with little prudence and planning but a heavy dose of Walt's can-do attitude, they rashly opened, with the money Walt had saved while serving in France, their own business: Iwerks-Disney Commercial Artists. Finding customers, however, proved difficult, and when

A Walt Disney advertisement from a business envelope, Kansas City, Missouri, 1921.

Walt decided to supplement his income by taking a side job with the Kansas City Slide Company, which introduced him to the budding business of commercial film production, the Iwerks-Disney company quickly ran aground. Ub had neither the talent nor the temperament to manage a company, and within two months of its opening, the joint venture had failed.

Walt and Ub then went to work full-time for the slide company, which had changed its name to the Kansas City Film Ad Company. It was then that Walt's next big idea was suddenly hatched: he and Ub would create, for the many movie theaters that were opening throughout the country, a series of one- and two-minute animated cartoons called Laugh-O-Grams. Upon selling their first film in 1921 to the local Newman Theater, the most opulent theater in Kansas City, the young men decided once again to open their own company, this one called Laugh-O-Gram Films. Giddy on the sip of their first success, they signed with a distributor in 1922. As happened before, problems followed in short order. The distributor promised much but delivered little, and when coupled with Disney's under-assessment of production costs, it wasn't long before the troika—Walt, Ub, and the distributor—were bankrupt. Walt was now in dire straits. His family had since moved away, and he was living on restaurant credits and canned beans, sleeping on the floor of his studio next to his drawing board, and visiting the train station once a week to get a hot bath for a dime. "It was probably the blackest time of my life," he wrote.

Although dejected and broke, Walt was never broken in spirit, and he remained confident that he was destined for a career in film and animation. But his passion didn't blind him to reality:

he faced a crossroads and needed a new path to reach his goal. Geography, he concluded, was clearly his enemy, for the new path that beckoned led him from Kansas City to the heart of the nascent film industry—Hollywood. So with $40 in his pocket and a frayed cardboard suitcase, Walt headed west in July 1923. "It was a big day, the day I got on that Santa Fe California Limited [train] . . . I was just free and happy," he wrote. Although he acknowledged "I'd failed," he was quick to find the silver lining: "I think it's important to have a good hard failure when you're young. . . . I learned a lot out of that." And, he added with a sense of accomplishment: "I never felt sorry for myself."

Upon arriving in Hollywood, Walt joined forces with his older brother Roy and started milking their contacts, sending out samples of Walt's work, until finally landing a contract for six of Walt's "Alice Comedies," which featured a live-action little girl against an animated landscape. Invigorated by the contract, Walt and Roy opened on October 16, 1923, the Disney Brothers Cartoon Studio, marking the official start of the Disney Company. Iwerks soon joined them in California, and together they released in 1927 their first fully animated short films featuring a mischievous character called Oswald the Lucky Rabbit. Produced for Universal Studios, the character became a star, even rivalling the popular Felix the Cat and inspiring a line of Oswald-related merchandise and candy bars. But when Disney traveled to New York in February 1928 to renegotiate a bigger advance on the Oswald films to offset (once

"You may not realize it when it happens, but a kick in the teeth may be the best thing in the world for you."

WALT DISNEY

again) higher-than-expected production costs, his distributor not only refused to offer a higher payment but even offered *less* per cartoon. Outraged, Disney rejected the new terms, whereupon his distributor simply hired away Walt's team of animators (all of them except Iwerks) and began producing the Oswald films for Universal himself, which he could do because Disney had failed to protect the rights to his character. (If vengeance is a dish best served cold, then the Disney Company's must have been dry iced, for it eventually did regain the rights to Oswald—78 years later, in 2006.)

Walt, again, was left with nothing. If he had, at that moment, finally pronounced the death of his flatlining career in art and animation, no one would have blamed him. After all, how many failures could a young man suffer before concluding what would have seemed obvious to many: that his life was on the wrong track, and that his future lay elsewhere. But such defeatism was never something Disney could countenance; it ran against every fiber of his being. In fact, according to Walt, it was during his dejected train ride back to Hollywood from his distributor's office in New York that he generated the idea that would change his life—and the course of film history and popular culture as well. The new character he imagined was patterned after a rodent that had lived in his old office at the Film Ad Company in Kansas City. "Mice gathered in my wastebasket when I worked late at night," he recalled. "I lifted them out and kept them in little cages on my desk. One of them was particularly friendly." That "friend" became the basis of Walt's new character, and by the end of the train ride, according to Walt, he had not only sketched out the character's appearance (which in reality was just a clever redrawing of Oswald the Rabbit) but even thought up the plot for the character's first cartoon adventure. Walt named his creation Mortimer Mouse, a name hated by his wife. To her, the character's name was all wrong and sounded "too sissy." So Walt took her advice and rechristened his character with a more endearing name, "Mickey."

Mickey starred in two silent films before Disney cleverly employed, in November 1928, the novelty of synchronized sound (sound that matched the action of the characters on the screen) for the third Mickey production. The result—*Steamboat Willie*—became a landmark event in cultural history. Directed, produced, and voiced by Disney, it was the first megahit "talkie" animated film, paving the way for Disney's dominance in animation and Mickey's rise to fame as one of the most recognizable figures in the world.

Mickey's cheerful optimism and plucky demeanor in the face of adversity mirrored the spunk and moxie of his maker, and he proved to be the perfect antidote to the anxieties of the Depression. In fact, Mickey's celebrity and influence seemingly knew no bounds. By the end of 1930, as biographer Neal Gabler pointed out, a Mickey Mouse comic strip had been syndicated in 40 newspapers in 22 countries, generating for Disney $1,500 each month; by the end of 1931, more than 30 Mickey films had been released, and a "Mickey Mouse Club" had attracted one million members; by the end of 1932, a Mickey Mouse cartoon and Walt had each received an Academy Award; by the end of 1933, some 900,000 Mickey Mouse watches and clocks and ten million Mickey ice cream cones had been sold; by 1934, Walt was receiving some $600,000 a year from his films and merchandising, with the latter now earning more than the former (establishing a blueprint to *real* riches that would revolutionize Hollywood); and in 1935, the League of Nations, the forerunner of the United Nations, even honored Walt with a gold medal, proclaiming Mickey "a symbol of universal good will." From art and animation, film and television, the vacation and travel industry, education and play and the marriage of the two, to the whole novelty and notion of family entertainment, to say nothing of corporate branding, advertising, and merchandising—there are few sectors of modern culture and corporate life anywhere in the world untouched in some way by the extraordinary shadow of Disney's seminal mouse. Disney critics would later castigate this global influence as cultural imperialism, but Disney and his supporters had a simpler name for it: success.

Such stunning achievement did not, however, mean smooth sailing for Disney. The struggle to reconcile his penchant for perfectionism with skyrocketing production costs, coupled with the anxiety of his home life in the wake of his wife's miscarriage, proved too much for him, and he suffered a nervous breakdown in 1931. Further pressure followed, when public skepticism accompanied his plan for a full-length animated feature film, a venture panned by critics as "Disney's Folly." But Disney realized like no other pioneer before him what the possibilities could be for his particular art form, and so despite the sneers and jeers from the press and movie insiders, he pushed on with his dream and vision of the future, finally releasing on December 21, 1937, the groundbreaking *Snow White and*

the Seven Dwarfs. The film, made from 2 million drawings by a crew of 600 people at a cost of $1.5 million (during the depths of the Depression), proved to be the perfect outlet not only for Disney's unwavering grit—his tireless passion and perseverance—but also for his amazing organizational abilities and capacity for hard work. Instead of the boondoggle of a flop that his detractors had predicted, *Snow White* became the highest-grossing movie of its day, acclaimed by critics as a genuine work of art. With the profits from the film, Disney financed the building of a multimillion-dollar studio in Burbank, California, where Disney Studios remain today.

Clara Barton

Born: December 25, 1821, Oxford, Massachusetts
Died: April 12, 1912, Glen Echo, Maryland

CHAPTER 9

The Hard Path Unpaved

Clara Barton

B y the time the sun set on September 17, 1862, some 23,000 soldiers were dead, wounded, or missing in Antietam, Maryland—it was the bloodiest single day of war in American history. On this Civil War battlefield and many others, and at nearby barns and houses that served as field hospitals, a little, nondescript woman in a bonnet and long dress worked tirelessly to relieve the suffering. Amid gunfire, cannons, the smoky chaos of battle, the hideous smell of the unburied, and the heart-wrenching cries and whimperings of the wounded, she quietly and efficiently did anything that anyone might need. She located and delivered medical supplies, cooked hot meals for the troops, hand-fed the helpless, bandaged the bleeding, blanketed the freezing, wrote letters for soldiers, read to them, recorded their dying words, noted their names for posterity, closed the eyes of the perished, prayed over their bodies, prepped others for surgery, assisted with amputations, set up lanterns so that surgeons could work throughout the night, and even cleared and cleaned the operating-room floors that were laden with severed limbs, blood, and excrement. On one occasion, while cradling the head of a wounded soldier on the battlefield to give him a drink, a bullet passed through the sleeve of her dress and into the man's chest, killing him instantly; on another, a soldier shot in the face insisted that she extract the bullet herself, since the surgeons were busy. She complied, cutting free the bullet with her pocket knife. "My business," she said simply, "is staunching blood, and feeding fainting men."

As Army surgeon James Dunn wrote, "In my feeble estimation, General McClellan [commander of the Union forces], with all his laurels, sinks into insignificance besides the true heroine of the age, the angel of the battlefield," Clara Barton.

News of Clara's heroic actions spread from battlefield to battlefield during the American Civil War. Soldiers in hospitals applauded her when she entered, and her mere presence could raise the soldiers' spirits. But such fame didn't sit well with everyone, especially with many Union men of authority (and even some women) who were dead set against ladies being anywhere near a battlefield, even as nurses and volunteers. Only after great pleading with military and civilian officials was she finally allowed access to the front lines and field hospitals.

Clara, in fact, would spend the better part of her life treading terrain where women had never been or had never been welcomed, and the unpaved trail she blazed was hard indeed. As a child, the tomboyish Clara was exceptionally bright—she was reading by age three—and she especially adored her father, a veteran of the Indian campaigns of the late 18th and early 19th centuries and the source of her lifelong interest in the military; for hours she would sit at her father's feet, listening to his tales about fighting the Indians and defeating the great warrior Tecumseh alongside future president William Henry Harrison. But outside their circle of family and friends, Clara suffered from a near paralytic shyness, a condition hardly ameliorated by her genetic fate—she was short, homely, and plump and spoke with a lisp. Her parents tried many things to conquer her inhibitions. They first sent her to a boarding school—with disastrous results. Clara recoiled at such drastic change and devolved into a deep depression. When she finally stopped eating, growing weak from what today would likely be diagnosed as anorexia, she was returned home on doctor's orders. Concerned, desperate, and frustrated, her parents then turned for help to that foremost quackery of 19th-century science and medicine: head-reading, otherwise known as phrenology. They consulted the most celebrated American noggin-reader of the day, the itinerant skull doctor Lorenzo Fowler, who on the basis of his "scientific" analysis of the shape of Clara's head concluded that what the child needed most was a dose of tough love. The absurdity of his methods notwithstanding (phrenology is "the science of picking the pocket through the scalp," quipped the acid-tongued Ambrose Bierce), Fowler's diagnosis was surprisingly sound. So the teenage Clara was forced out of the home and into a profession, teaching. The prospect of standing in front of a room of utter strangers petrified Clara—especially when the students were nearly her own age and often larger than she in size and spirit—but it proved to be the turning point of her life. For despite her fears and inhibitions, she quickly discovered through teaching and her service to others a sense of purpose and self-worth otherwise lacking in her life. Only one other time had she experienced such joy and satisfaction: it was during the two years she had spent caring for her brother left bedridden from a fall, when she rarely left his side, attended to his every need, and even applied leeches to his body as part of the silly and even harmful bloodletting regimen recommended by his doctors. Such service foreshadowed her Civil War mission to come.

So Barton became a teacher—in fact, a *wonderful* teacher—and with her confidence brimming, she even established her own school, in Bordentown, New Jersey, in 1852. It was the state's first free public school, and it grew from six students to hundreds in a single year. Clara's institution became so successful that the town's male leaders took the next logical step given the milieu of the times: they elected a male principal to run it, at more than twice Clara's salary, demoting her to his "female assistant." Infuriated and crushed by the move, Clara quit. Other teaching opportunities came her way, but she rejected them all because they failed to offer a salary commensurate with her male colleagues. "I may sometimes be willing to teach for nothing," she said, "but if paid at all, I shall never do a man's work for less than a man's pay." It was this principled pride that made Barton in coming years such an attractive model for the leaders of the early women's rights movement.

Despite the painful way this experience ended, Clara had accomplished much during this period in her life. Most importantly, she had conquered the timorous ways of her youth and fortified a faith in her own abilities, even mustering the courage to uproot and relocate to Washington, D.C. There, in 1854, she landed a position with the U.S. Patent Office, becoming one of the first women to work for the federal government. But here, again, the bright and competent Clara quickly ran afoul of the gender politics of the day. Calling her a "pest in petticoats," a cabal of men in the office conspired against her, spitting tobacco juice at her, blowing smoke in her face, and spreading nefarious rumors about her supposed promiscuity. (Clara would never marry, though she did have male suitors.) This time, despite the harassment, Clara refused to quit and worked there for several years.

But it was Clara's subsequent Civil War experience—tied to names now synonymous with that most uncivil of wars, such as Bull Run, Chantilly, South Mountain, Antietam, Fredericks- burg, Charleston, Petersburg, and Cold Harbor—that would help make her a household name. Her war-related service, in fact, spanned not only the entirety of the war—beginning on the first days that followed the attack on Fort Sumter in April 1861, when she aided the Union troops who had been battered and bloodied by paving stones, wielded by Confederate sympathizers, as they passed through Baltimore en route to defend Washington, D.C.— but continued afterward, when she organized and managed, with the blessing of President Abraham Lincoln in the final weeks of his life, what came to be known as the Missing Soldiers Office. By 1868, with a team of assistants she hired at her own expense (Congress would later reimburse her $15,000), Barton had an- swered some 63,000 letters from families and friends of the missing and identified more than 22,000 soldiers, 13,000 of whom were found buried in anonymous graves at the infamous Confederate prisoner-of-war camp in Andersonville, Georgia. For organizing this herculean effort, she was henceforth hailed as the "Heroine of Andersonville."

Emotionally and physically fagged by almost a decade of war service (and by the lecture circuit she went on immediately after the war, when she shared the dais with such notables as Frederick Douglass, Ralph Waldo Emerson, and Mark Twain), Barton departed for Europe for a much-needed rest—only to find yet another war. In Strasbourg, Paris, and elsewhere in France, Barton would spend the next year helping soldiers and civilians left injured or impoverished by the Franco-Prussian War of 1870-71. It proved to be one of the most consequential experiences of her professional life, for there she witnessed a new organization in action, the International Red Cross. As Barton noted, the Red Cross staff accomplished "in four months under their systematic organization what we failed to accomplish [during the American Civil War] in four years without it—no mistakes, no needless suffering, no starving, no lack of care, no waste, no confusion, but order, plenty, cleanliness and comfort." It was then and there that she decided to push for a branch of the Red Cross in America.

The International Red Cross required that each new chapter be recognized by its national government, which in turn needed to ratify the Geneva Convention of 1864 that protected the right of neutral medical personnel to aid the sick and wounded during wartime. But the United States was not a party to the Geneva Convention, and so Barton began to lobby the "powers that be." She blanketed Capitol Hill, visiting senators and representatives, and eventual met with President Rutherford B. Hayes. But despite her charm and passionate pleas, her efforts came up dry. Sheer earnestness would not be enough this time.

Her efforts failed because the president and others saw the Red Cross, an international *wartime* agency, as an unnecessary "entangling alliance" that was hardly needed given the unlikelihood of another war on American soil. Although Barton hated to admit it, the objection was a fair one. Clearly, if Barton were going to succeed this time, she needed a new plan.

As mentioned earlier, strategic shifts in pursuit of one's goals were a common weapon in the arsenal of these masters of grit—simply surrendering in the face of obstacles was never an option. So just as Ruth Handler would do in the wake of Barbie's disastrous debut, Barton would do as well: she would craft a bold change. But whereas Handler would revolutionize her marketing and not change her product, Barton would maintain her method of marketing—her prodding, persistence, and endless pestering—but revolutionize her product: she would fundamentally change the Red Cross mission itself. For why, Barton asked, couldn't this wonderful army of organized mercy, which had performed such miracles on the battlefield, also be useful during peacetime emergencies, aiding the victims of such disasters as famines, floods, fires, and earthquakes? Whether the enemy is armed soldiers or the forces of nature, weren't the victims of their fury just as worthy of our care?

European organizers of the Red Cross had suggested this idea many years before, but their efforts had gone for naught. The gritty Barton, however, had a penchant for succeeding where others had failed, and with her clever retooling of the agency's mission she not only won government support for the Red Cross in America (the U.S. Senate finally ratified the Geneva Convention in 1882) but transformed the Red Cross movement itself. Called the "American Amendment" in honor of Barton's efforts, this expansion of the Red Cross mission from wartime service into disaster relief was officially adopted by the organization at its international conference in Geneva, Switzerland, in 1884.

Barton spent the next two decades as the first president of the American Red Cross, aiding the needy at home and abroad. She spent the 1880s organizing relief for drought-stricken Texas, tornado-wracked Illinois, yellow fever-plagued Florida, fire-razed Michigan, and flood-ravaged Ohio and Pennsylvania (where the catastrophic Johnstown Flood had killed 2,200). In 1893, she went to the rescue of the Sea Islands off the coast of South Carolina, where a hurricane had left thousands dead or homeless. In 1896, she traveled to Turkey to aid the victims of the Armenian famine and massacres; in 1898, she went to Cuba to organize civilian relief, orphanages, and medical assistance (to injured Cubans and Theodore Roosevelt's wounded Rough Riders) during the Spanish-American War; and in 1900, she organized a massive relief effort in Galveston, Texas, where on September 8, a 135-145 mph hurricane,

"I have an almost complete disregard of precedent, and a faith in the possibility of something better. It irritates me to be told how things have always been done. I defy the tyranny of precedent."

CLARA BARTON

with 15-foot storm surges, killed some 6,000 people and perhaps as many as 12,000—the deadliest natural disaster in American history.

This last effort was especially taxing on the nearly 80-year-old Barton, who worked tirelessly for months in stifling heat and humidity amid the matchstick remains of the island city. The burning of bodies—the corpses had initially been buried at sea, but the tides repeatedly washed them back ashore—continued

Rummaging through the rubble in the wake of the September 8, 1900, hurricane that destroyed Galveston, Texas, and killed 6,000-12,000 people. The deadliest natural disaster in American history, it was also Clara Barton's last major field operation as head of the American Red Cross.

into November, and the stench of burning flesh permeated the air. What Barton contributed in Galveston during these grim and desperate times, both in leadership and in material relief, was incalculable. She organized homes for the homeless, established orphanages for the now parentless, bought and distributed 1.5 million strawberry plants to destitute farmers who were desperate for a cash crop, and leveraged her celebrity status to focus national and even international attention on the disaster, spurring much-needed donations of food, money, and supplies. Some of her efforts had lasting social and political significance as well. When she assigned a woman to each of the city's 12 wards to oversee relief and rebuilding efforts, she gave them an unprecedented amount of political power. As Patricia Bixel and Elizabeth Turner wrote in *Galveston and the 1900 Storm,* local women saw in Barton and her take-charge attitude "a powerful and effective humanitarian, who in no way 'unsexed' herself by assuming a masculine demeanor. She demonstrated that a woman could lead and still be a woman." Moreover, to ensure a fair distribution of relief supplies (always a challenge), Barton founded an African American auxiliary to the Red Cross, to which she gave money directly for spending as it saw fit, thereby minimizing the possibility of discrimination by the white middlemen in charge of distributing relief supplies. Local blacks were certainly at a disadvantage during the disaster. When not enough men could be found for the gathering and burning of the thousands of corpses and animal carcasses that were rapidly decomposing—pyres smoldered throughout the city for this grisly but necessary task—local "volunteers" were rounded up at gunpoint and by bayonet. The most common "volunteers"? Resident blacks.

This concern for equal treatment was no passing whim for Barton. Two years earlier, she had resigned as honorary president of the National Society of the Spanish War upon learning that African Americans were banned from the organization; and as part of her hurricane-relief mission to the Sea Islands in 1893-4, she had spent some ten months aiding the poor and predominantly African American population.

The Galveston mission was Barton's last major field action, and the strenuous undertaking left her bedridden for a month. But Barton recovered, and in 1902 she even traveled as far as St. Petersburg, Russia, where she led the U.S. delegation to the Seventh International Conference of the Red Cross and was feted as one of the leading humanitarians in the world. In 1904, however, amid increasingly nasty obloquy about her advanced age and highly personal style of management, which were seen as liabilities for the growing and increasingly professionalized agency, Barton was forced to step down as Red Cross president. Although angered and hurt by her ouster from the very organization she had created, Barton obstinately refused to retire from public life and simply found a new outlet for her humanitarian zeal. In 1905 she established the National First Aid Association of America—stressing emergency preparedness, developing first aid kits, and forming ambulance brigades for police and fire departments—and served as its honorary president for the next five years.

Upon her death in Glen Echo, Maryland, in 1912, at age 90, Barton was transported back home for burial in Massachusetts. When the driver of the horse-drawn carriage carrying her casket to a waiting train learned the identity of his distinguished passenger, he dropped his reins in amazement. The driver's father, a *Confederate* soldier, had been shot in the throat during the Battle of Antietam, and the little, nondescript woman in the bonnet and long dress who had bandaged his wound and saved his life had been none other than the "angel of the battlefield."

Abraham Lincoln

Born: February 12, 1809, near Hodgenville, Kentucky
Died: April 15, 1865, Washington, D.C.

CHAPTER 10

Slips, Not Falls

Abraham Lincoln

Good looks matter, or at least that was the lesson widely gleaned from that historic night in Chicago in 1960, when John Kennedy, the dapper junior senator from Massachusetts, looked cool and confident ("telegenic" would become the chic term) and Richard Nixon, the vice president, appeared sweaty and sick. Whereas Kennedy, during this first televised broadcast of a presidential debate, gazed straight into the camera and addressed the public with a sense of purpose, demonstrating the political power of this still nascent medium, Nixon avoided the lens, seemed uneasy with the camera, and looked shifty and unsettled. The magnetic young senator, it turns out, had spent the days prior to the debate holed up in a hotel, relaxing and fielding question after question in preparation for the big night. Nixon, by contrast, had recently been hospitalized with an injured knee, was suffering from the flu, was running a fever, had visibly lost weight, was exhausted from "campaign cramming" to make up for lost time, and had even reinjured his bad leg upon arriving for the debate when he accidently banged it on the door of his limo. Proving that bad situations could always be worse, Nixon then compounded his problems and the negative "optics" of the evening by wearing both a light-colored suit, which only accentuated his already ashen appearance, and a pancake-size layer of Lazy Shave, a drugstore makeup intended to hide his notorious five o'clock shadow (his "menacing mug") but which caused him to sweat profusely in front of the TV studio lights. "My God," said Chicago mayor Richard J. Daley upon seeing Nixon that night, "they've embalmed him before he even died." Nixon's running mate, Henry Cabot Lodge, Jr., had a more personal, pressing, and political take on the evening: "That son of a bitch just lost the election."

Now, whether good looks alone can win someone an election, or even just a debate, is highly questionable. But there is no denying that, for good or ill, personal appearances matter, and they always have mattered, especially in politics where image can be king.

Take Abraham Lincoln, for example. A more arresting individual in his day could hardly have been found, not least because of his unusual height. True, the Kentucky-born boy from the prairie was impressively tall, but he was *unnervingly* so. At a time when the average height of an adult male was about five feet, six inches, Lincoln towered at seven feet when wearing his beloved stovepipe hat. Moreover, his sad-sack appearance (his "melancholy," folks called it) was more depressing than inspiring, and the tortured land-scape of his face—so mapped and measured in his day by another technological marvel of political force, photography—featured sallow, sunken cheeks, a ruddy, crooked nose, an inflated lower lip, and cavernous eyes amid dark lines and crevices that conveyed more weakness and struggle than strength. Furthermore, his head, ears, hands, and feet appeared strangely oversized, giving rise to speculation among historians in the next century whether Lincoln suffered from a genetic disorder called Marfan syndrome. In fact, his arms and legs were so bony and lengthy that his secretary of war, Edwin Stanton, called him a "damned long-armed ape" (a not uncommon comparison once the hirsute Lincoln became America's first bearded president). To make matters worse, Lincoln stood with a stoop, inclined his head forward, and walked steadily but slowly in a weird, halting way, lifting "his foot all at once, not lifting himself from the toes, and hence had no spring or snap . . . to his walk," as his law partner William Herndon noted; and when he spoke in public, "there is an involuntary comical awkwardness which marks his movements," reported the *New-York Tribune,* and "a frequent tendency to dwindle into a shrill and unpleasant sound." Although Lincoln's rather high-pitched voice could still carry a crowd, his speech and sound were strange and startling and much less commanding than expected from this larger-than-life figure.

Lincoln's manner of dress only added to his abject ungainliness. As historian Richard Current suggested, if clothes make the man, they *unmade* this man, which is seldom an asset for a politician. Young Abe was an especially easy target of ridicule, the kind of pitiful prey whom cyberbullies and body-shamers would devour today. Girls teased and taunted the tousled-haired giant without mercy, calling him as "thin as a beanpole and as ugly as a scarecrow." Other observers compared him to a dressed-up skeleton, and an oafish one at that given his fondness for a single suspender to keep his pants from falling down. Nor would Lincoln's sartorial savviness improve with age. English journalist Edward Dicey, as cited by Current, said Lincoln's suit was "unfashionably tight, creased in the wrong places, and also soiled," and that his "pants were too short and the gloves too long—too long even for his bony fingers." Nathaniel Hawthorne noted Lincoln's "shabby slippers" and "rusty black frock coat and pantaloons." Even at Lincoln's brilliant Cooper Union speech in February 1860, which many see as the pivotal event that sealed his nomination for president and eventual victory in the general election, his shabby attire drew fire. As one commentator noted, his suit was "evidently the work of an unskilled tailor."

Lincoln freely acknowledged the liability of his looks. When Stephen Douglas, during one of his famous debates with Lincoln, accused the future president of being two-faced, Lincoln memorably quipped, "Honestly, if I were two-faced, would I be showing you this one?" On yet another occasion, when Lincoln learned that his always testy secretary of war had progressed from calling him an ape to a baboon and a fool, Lincoln took the news with faux astonishment. Other leaders might have sacked a subaltern guilty of such insolence or at least reproached him, but not Lincoln. What bothered him, he said, was not Stanton's comments but that Stanton had a penchant for being right.

And it was exactly in this manner—with his self-deprecating humor and humility, along with his calm, compassion, charm, sincerity, decisiveness, and eloquence—that Lincoln countered the deck so obviously stacked against him, rose above the unflattering figure he cut, and warmed audiences large and small, both political and personal, to his favor. "He knew that he was ugly, ungainly, awkward in society," noted the great polymath and pedagogue Jacques Barzun, but "he did not resent these deficiencies [and]

Abraham Lincoln, with General George McClellan (second from left), on the battlefield at Antietam, Maryland, October 3, 1962. This photo by Alexander Gardner clearly shows Lincoln's commanding stature in relation to other men of his day.

neither tried to cover them up nor referred to them continually from embarrassment. They were part of him . . . as a fact of nature." In other words, Lincoln had learned early on to accept himself as he was, startling stature and mannerisms and all, and from this acceptance he gained strength, confidence, and even leverage over others who might otherwise have turned his deficiencies against him. For Lincoln, his "liabilities" ranked among his dearest assets.

Recognizing Lincoln's special qualities, however, was no instantaneous epiphany moment. He was still too imposing, too gawky, too utterly different to negate the very strange shadow he immediately cast. Like the photoreceptors of our eyes that need time to transition from darkness to light, some period of adjustment was apparently needed to first scan and take in the totality of this walking, talking idiosyncrasy of a man. But according to Lincoln scholar Harold Holzer, this interlude was brief:

> They all [firsthand accounts] seem to say, for the first ten minutes I couldn't believe the way he looked, the way he sounded, his accent. But after ten minutes, the flash of his eyes, the ease of his presentation overcame all doubts, and I was enraptured. . . . I am paraphrasing, but there is ten minutes of saying, what the heck is that, and then all of a sudden it's the ideas that supersede whatever flaws there are.

The German-born Union Army officer Carl Schurz sounded a similar note in Lincoln's day, highlighting the deceptive nature of first impressions when it came to Lincoln:

He is indeed a man without higher education and his manners harmonize little with the European conception of the dignity of a ruler. . . . He is an overgrown nature-child and does not understand artifices of speech and attitude. But he is a man of profound feeling, just and firm principles, and incorruptible integrity. One can always rely upon his motives, and the characteristic gift of this people, a sound common sense, is developed in him to a marvelous degree.

However, even with the benefit of these manifold gifts, Lincoln faced difficulties at every turn. His rise from local to state and then national prominence was a miraculous achievement, especially for a dirt-poor boy from a log cabin whose education consisted of less than one year of formal schooling and a self-study of the Bible, Shakespeare, assorted textbooks, and world classics. But his path to greatness was never certain—there was nothing preordained about it—and it certainly wasn't free of the frequent stain of defeat.

Lincoln's litany of failures and tribulations is legendary. In 1832, he ran for a seat in the Illinois legislature and lost. In 1833, he and a partner opened a business that swiftly went bankrupt and left him deeply in debt. He was elected to the Illinois House of Representatives in 1834 but then suffered a nervous breakdown the following year when his beloved sweetheart (Ann Rutledge) died and left him severely depressed if not suicidal. He successfully earned his

"Always bear in mind that your own resolution to succeed, is more important than any other one thing."

ABRAHAM LINCOLN

law license in 1836 but then lost his bid for the Illinois Speaker of the House in 1838 and suffered another emotional break in 1841 when he ended his engagement to Mary Todd, his eventual wife. He lost his bid for a seat in the U.S. House of Representatives in 1843, but after finally winning a U.S House seat three years later, he then served only one term. In 1849, he lost the one case he argued before the U.S. Supreme Court (though he argued some 175 cases before the Illinois Supreme Court) and was even defeated in his attempt to become a land officer in Illinois. He lost a bid for the U.S. Senate in 1854, lost his bid for the Vice Presidential nomination in 1856, lost his run for the U.S. Senate in 1858, and then, in 1861, upon finally reaching the highest political office in the land, his election to the presidency destroyed the Union and plunged the nation into a devastating civil war, one of the bloodiest in history, that cost, in proportion to today's population, some eight million Americans their lives.

Moreover, Lincoln was widely deified in the tomb by those who had detested him in the flesh, a fact easily forgotten given the polished lens of reverence through which he is generally viewed today. (Mark Bowden of *The Atlantic* recounts this rich history of anti-Lincoln vitriol in the wonderfully titled essay, "'Idiot,' 'Yahoo,' 'Original Gorilla': How Lincoln Was Dissed in His Day.") In fact, Lincoln and his wartime leadership were roundly anathematized by not only opposition Democrats but also members of his own party, be they rabid Abolitionists or racist whites wedded to the status quo. The racial tightrope of moderation and conciliation that Lincoln maneuvered, balancing principle with the necessary burden of pragmatism, may seem prudent and praiseworthy in hindsight, but his policies infuriated many and satisfied few at the time. Even the Gettysburg Address, now ranked among the greatest orations in history, was excoriated in its day. As the London *Times* reported on the two-minute event, "Anything more dull and commonplace it wouldn't be easy to produce." Newspapers closer to home were harsher still. "We pass over the silly remarks of the President," declared the *Patriot & Union*, published just 40 miles from Gettysburg, in Harrisburg, Pennsylvania. "For the credit of the nation we are willing that the veil of oblivion shall be dropped over them and that they shall be no more repeated or thought of." Only with Lincoln's own death—his martyrdom, as many would come to view his assassination on Good Friday, 1865—would this horrific chapter in American history begun with his presidency and this tortuous period for him personally (he would even bury two sons, one in 1850, another in 1862) finally come to a close.

Few leaders in history have ever faced such peaks and valleys of triumph and tragedy and such enormous pressure and strain, and many others would have faltered under the burdens and given up far earlier on the long and weary road that Lincoln traveled. But despite such daunting adversity—the seemingly endless disappointments that he suffered in his public life and the dark periods of depression that he battled in private—Lincoln would never be utterly incapacitated by grief or allow himself to slide permanently into an all-consuming, paralyzing self-pity. Instead, the adversity seemed only to double his resolve and grit. For through force of will and constant self-reflection, Lincoln gleaned from his struggles a larger purpose to his life, forging from his anguish critical skills and capacities for surviving and persevering that left him, his ambition, and his faith in providence and his destiny all the stronger in the end. "It's a slip not a fall," he told himself after losing the hard-fought senate race to Stephen Douglas in 1858. And just a slip it was, for despite the painful loss, Lincoln had snatched from the jaws of this crushing defeat something more powerful than a seat in the U.S. Senate: he had become a national household name, and this left him well positioned to win the Republican nomination for the presidency two years later.

In other words, Lincoln dealt with adversities as he dealt with his physical deficiencies. They were not enemies to vanquish but realities to accept, endure, and, if possible, even bend to one's favor. As writer Joshua Wolf Shenk put it, "The suffering [Lincoln] endured lent him clarity and conviction, creative skills in the face of adversity, and a faithful humility that helped him guide the nation through its greatest perils."

So by learning from his failures, accepting his limitations, drawing meaning from his struggles, and enduring his shortcomings and "blue spells" with humor, humility, and an offsetting appreciation for life's simple pleasures and diversions—a good book, a funny story, and the comforting presence of family, friends, even pets—Lincoln navigated a most improbable path. Although fated with a pedigree unpromising and unmoneyed, this most earnestly self-made of self-made men rose from poverty to the presidency with a dogged resolve and a belief in his destiny that Herndon likened to "a little engine that knew no rest"; or to change the metaphor, Lincoln mastered the ability to soldier on, with patience and purpose, against all odds, through crisis after crisis, often forlorn but not defeated, living to fight another day on yet another front until finally reaching the hallowed realm where he resides today: as the Savior of the Union, the Great Emancipator of the enslaved, and to many the greatest president in American history.

"I love [Lincoln] not because he was perfect," said W.E.B. Du Bois, the foremost civil rights leader in the United States in the first half of the 20th century, "but because he was not and yet triumphed."